CW01303817

Make it easily!
BREAD BASIC BAKING GUIDE

FOR BEGINNERS

Homemade Yeast and Yeast-Free
Easy-to-Bake Bread Recipes

Sarah Ray

©Copyright 2020 by Sarah Ray - All rights reserved. This document is geared towards providing exact and reliable information in regards to the topic and issue covered. The publication is sold with the idea that the publisher is not required to render accounting, officially permitted, or otherwise, qualified services. If advice is necessary, legal or professional, a practiced individual in the profession should be ordered. From a Declaration of Principles which was accepted and approved equally by a Committee of the American Bar Association and a Committee of Publishers and Associations. In no way is it legal to reproduce, duplicate, or transmit any part of this document in either electronic means or in printed format. Recording of this publication is strictly prohibited and any storage of this document is not allowed unless with written permission from the publisher. All rights reserved. The information provided herein is stated to be truthful and consistent, in that any liability, in terms of inattention or otherwise, by any usage or abuse of any policies, processes, or directions contained within is the solitary and utter responsibility of the recipient reader. Under no circumstances will any legal responsibility or blame be held against the publisher for any reparation, damages, or monetary loss due to the information herein, either directly or indirectly. Respective authors own all copyrights not held by the publisher. The information herein is offered for informational purposes solely, and is universal as so. The presentation of the information is without contract or any type of guarantee assurance. The trademarks that are used are without any consent, and the publication of the trademark is without permission or backing by the trademark owner. All trademarks and brands within this book are for clarifying purposes only and are the owned by the owners themselves, not affiliated with this document.

Sarah Ray. Make It Easily! Bread Basic Baking Guide for Beginners.
Homemade Yeast and Yeast-Free Easy-to-Bake Bread Recipes.
Full Color Print Edition.

Content

Content 6
Introduction 9
Important Terms 11
What Equipment Do You Need? 17
What Is Flour? 23
    Traditional Types of Flour 25
    Non-Traditional Types of Flour 26
Yeast Leavened Bread-Making Process 33
    7 Step Yeast Bread Baking Process 35
What You Should Know About a Starter 41
    How to Grow a Starter in 6 Days 45
    Storage of Starter Culture 50
    How to Feed a Starter 51
    How to Refresh a Sourdough Before Using it to Make Bread .. 53
    6 Starter Problems and Solutions 54
    Cure a Starter 60
Yeast Bread Recipes 63
    Sourdough Loaf Recipe 64
    Milk Bread Roll Recipe 70
    Rye Loaf Recipe 74
Bread-Making Process Non-Yeast Leavened 79
    Non-Yeast Bread Baking Process in 4 Steps 81
Yeast-Free Bread Recipes 83
    Soda Bread Recipe 84
    Cornbread Recipe – Gluten Free 88

Tortilla Recipe 92
Troubleshooting Tips 95
The Bread Didn't Work: 17 Reasons Why............................. 99
Conclusion 109
Bonus pages... 111
Relax pages... 119

Introduction

It started with a telephone call.

"Sarah, help me!" My friend, Sophia, blurted out in fright and despair. "It seems that your bread liquid wants to conquer my house!"

Let's be frank here. Baking bread is not as simple as mixing up flour, water, and yeast, throwing it into your oven, and expecting a perfect loaf to come out. Instead, it is an extensive and detailed process that requires patience and the ability to never to give up, even after you fail time and time again. But believe me, I have left no stone unturned so that when you read this book, you will ultimately pull out your first loaf of bread and surely be surprised with the stellar results.

Unfortunately, as a beginner who only knows how to scramble eggs, most of the guides available will only make the process seem harder, as they are aimed towards more experienced home cooks and professionals. That is why I decided on writing this book specifically aimed at beginners like you. This book will guide you with relevant, necessary details at each step, and is complete with handy troubleshooting tips to encourage you to bake your first loaf right at home. Being a housewife myself, I personally know the problems you would typically be facing, problems that most professional guides would not be able to solve.

I dedicate this book to my friend Sophia, a beautiful and creative person who is absolutely wonderful, but simultaneously doesn't understand anything about cooking, let alone baking bread. I remember how confusing the whole process seemed to her when she first started her journey.

She never understood the difference between a starter and yeast, like what each is, what they're for, and how they work in process of baking. Moreover, she was terrified by the word "autolyze," had no idea what a banneton looked like, and of course didn't know what type of flour was needed to get the best results for a particular kind of bread. After countless hours of trying to bake bread in her kitchen, including spilling several kilograms of flour, dozens of eggs, and a million cells of the nervous system, she soon gave up hope of ever baking a loaf of bread. That was when she came to me for guidance.

As a mother of three and an experienced housewife myself, for six years, I regularly baked bread for my family. Therefore, I felt the need to share my skills and experience with my dear Sophia, but also with you, my friend, in this book. I want to enable people with the simplest knowledge, newcomers to cooking, to touch this magic in order to learn the process of baking bread at home.

Bread-making is a highly flexible process where you are the master. You get to decide the timing, and that in itself is a great convenience while baking. I believe that bread-making is a fundamental part of cooking, and you don't have to be a professional to get great results. You only need to know the basics, in addition to some of the subtleties that I will share with you, and a little practice under my sensitive guidance in this book. In this book, you will find six easy recipes based on standard classic baking technologies. This is the basic knowledge that you need to start being familiar with, so that in the future, you will be able do everything. I painted the recipes with such detail that you simply have no chance of doing something wrong. Believe me, if my friend Sophia already pleases everyone in the district with her amazing bread, then you can too!

Important Terms

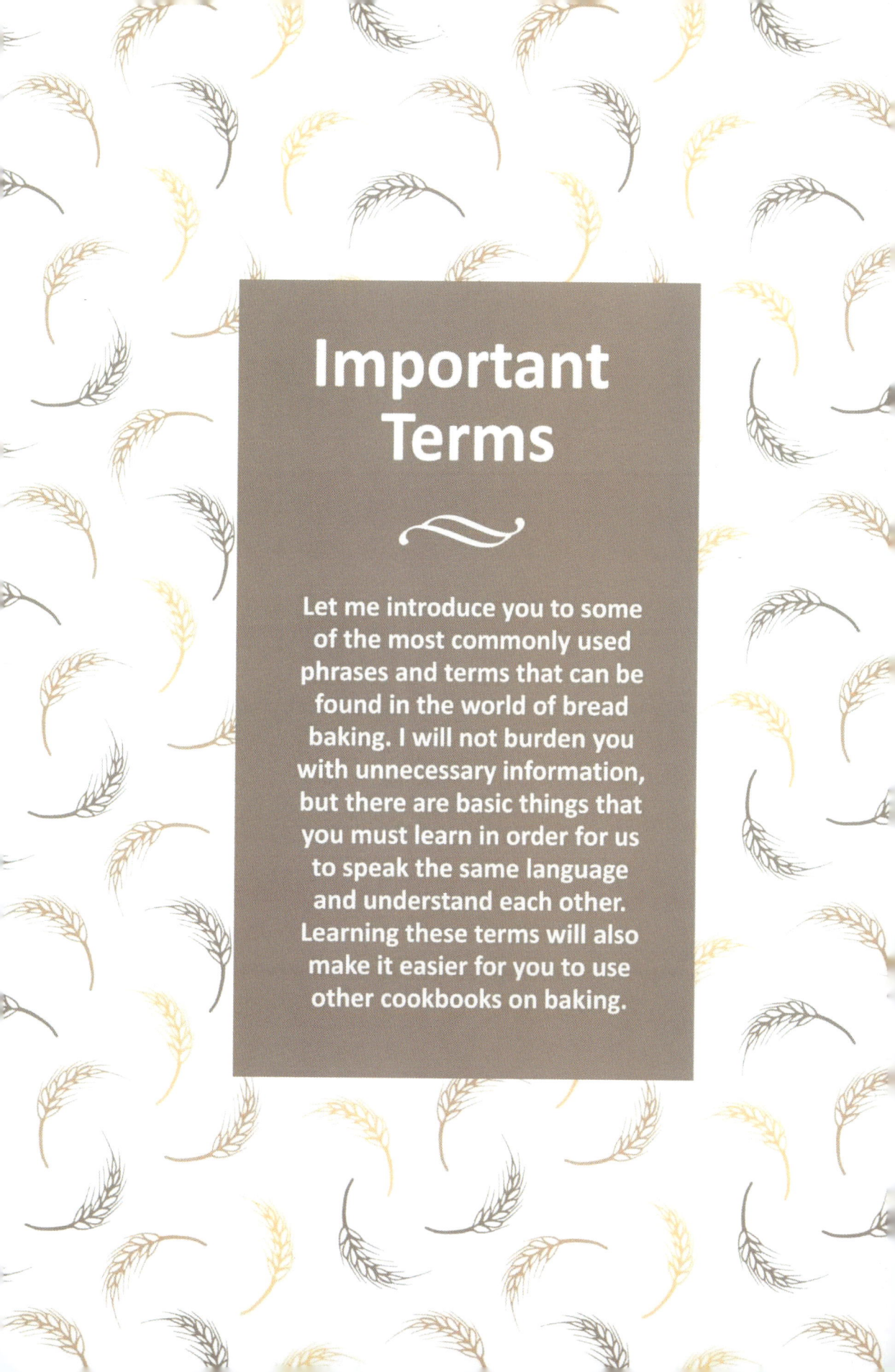

Let me introduce you to some of the most commonly used phrases and terms that can be found in the world of bread baking. I will not burden you with unnecessary information, but there are basic things that you must learn in order for us to speak the same language and understand each other. Learning these terms will also make it easier for you to use other cookbooks on baking.

Yeast: Yeasts are single-celled organisms. A by-product of the yeast's life is carbon dioxide, which is released in the form of tiny bubbles. These bubbles "get stuck" in the gluten carcass of the dough, forming a higher mesh and lush structure of the dough when baking.

Starter (sourdough, leaven): A starter is an analogue of yeast. Simply put, it is a bread leaven that is the base for many bakers. When the starter is ready, it contains a yeast, the microorganism responsible for fermenting your dough. This allows the dough to rise and also gives bread its airy texture. You can prepare a starter by either using commercial yeast (ready-made) or natural yeast (which is formed by fermentation of flour and water that we will make with our own hands). We will speak about this in more detail before we start the bread-making process.

Water roux (Tangzhong): is a paste of flour cooked in water or milk which is used to improve the texture of bread, making it soft and fluffy.

Crumb: This is the internal structure of the bread loaf. It may be light or dense, ultimately depending on the type of bread you bake.

Autolyze: Autolyze is the initial process of mixing flour and water before adding your starter. Usually, you will have to rest the mixture for some time, as specified in the recipe.

Hydration: Hydration is the baker's percentage of water present in the dough. Typically, the more the hydration, the stickier the dough, making it hard for inexperienced bakers to handle. But if you reduce the hydration, the dough will rise less.

Bulk Ferment (first fermentation, first rise): The resting phase of the dough after adding the starter and salt to the autolyze mixture is called bulk ferment. This process allows your starter's yeast to digest and transform the sugars in your dough to carbon, giving rise to a bubbly and light dough with a beautiful crumb. The amount of time spent on fermenting will decide the lightness of your dough, and also it varies from recipe to recipe. Bulk fermentation is the dough's first resting period that occurs after the yeast has been added and before the stage of shaping.

Proofing (final fermentation, final rise, second rise, blooming): This stage is the dough's final rise that happens after shaping and just before baking.

Gluten: Gluten is the protein responsible for ensuring the bread holds its shape. It makes up most of the bread's protein, and its development is vital for your bread's success.

Kneading: Kneading the dough is mixing the products described by the recipe until a homogeneous mass is obtained. This will have certain properties, such as dry or liquid, and elastic or solid. Kneading works the dough to develop gluten. Depending on the type of bread, you might need to work the dough continuously for a short period or slowly stretch and fold the dough at regular intervals for a more extended period of time. Refer to the recipe you're using for more information.

Shaping: Shaping is the process of tightening the gluten in the dough to form the desired shape of a loaf. It also allows the loaf to rise properly in the oven. Forming the bread is a very important and interesting step. There are many ways to shape your loaf, and we will discuss this further in the recipes. For example, there can be baguettes, loaves, pigtails, and various other types of bread molding. However, an unsuccessful shape can lead to problems with baking, with a crust (it can crack or "rip" it), and the bread can be inconvenient to cut into pieces and eat.

Boule: This is a traditional form of a round loaf taken up by the dough after the shaping process.

What Equipment Do You Need?

~

And so, let's take your first steps in the world of baking bread. But where to start? What do you need in order to try to make your first bread? I understand your concerns as a beginner, and I have done my best to explain all the tools you need to get you on your feet. In the absence of such equipment, I have pointed out several great alternatives that are readily available in your kitchen.

Glass Jar: Also known as a mason jar, a glass jar is used mainly used for storing preserves and jams. We will need this for growing and housing the starter for our bread. I recommend a jar with a capacity of half a liter or more.

Weighing Scale: Since bread-making is highly sensitive to the weight of ingredients added, you will need some form of accurate measurement. A kitchen weighing scale is simple to get your hands on and it guarantees the best results. If you cannot get one, you will need to measure in cups and approximate the weight. Refer to the conversion table at the end of the book for more information.

Mixing Bowl: These are large bowls with sloped edges allowing for the easy mixing of your ingredients and fermenting of your dough. You can substitute this with any large vessel that you have lying around.

Sieve: The flour sieve is a simple kitchen accessory. It has a peculiar body with a grill fixed on it. Despite its simplicity, this design is very effective. Various materials are used to produce the sieve. The most practical are products made of plastic and stainless steel.

Dutch Oven: A Dutch oven is an oval-shaped bowl with thick edges and a secure lid that is made from cast iron or ceramic. This is usually available online and make sure that it fits into your oven before purchasing. It mainly retains the moisture of the bread's environment while in the oven, preventing it from drying out quickly. If you cannot find or buy one, place the bread on a baking tray and add an ovenproof dish with some ice cubes underneath the bread while it bakes.

Measuring Cups and Spoons: As mentioned before, these will help you approximate the weight if you do not weigh using the scale. Keep in mind that liquid and dry cups are different from each other. Also, some recipes might specifically ask you to add the ingredient in cups or spoons, so keep these in hand. Since these are necessary, make sure to have the full set before starting.

Whisk: A whisk is a handy tool for mixing ingredients. You should have one lying around in your kitchen, but if you don't seem to have one on hand, you can easily purchase it online or at a nearby store.

Banneton: Also called a proofing basket, a banneton will be a place for your dough to rest during the proofing stage. It has having grooved edges to help your dough rise. If these are not available in your location, do not worry. You can substitute this with a mixing bowl or basket that has a clean kitchen towel on the inside and is also dusted with rice flour.

Spatula: A spatula is a spoon with a flat and flexible end, which is excellent for mixing up ingredients, especially for your starter. Make sure to have one that fits into your starter's glass jar to easily mix and fit inside.

Bench Scraper: An essential tool for ensuring a smooth operation, a bench scraper allows you to handle the dough without much effort and avoid sticky situations. You can also scrape off excess dough from your work area and divide your flour easily with this handy tool. Bench scrapers are either metal or plastic and are readily available online. In case you need an alternative, a flat rectangle piece of metal or plastic will do fine.

Oven Thermometer: This is a great tool that lets you identify the internal temperature of your bread and prevent over or undercooking. If you don't have access to a decent one, learn to tell the doneness by seeing the color of the crust or by inserting a toothpick and checking if it comes out clean.

What Is Flour?

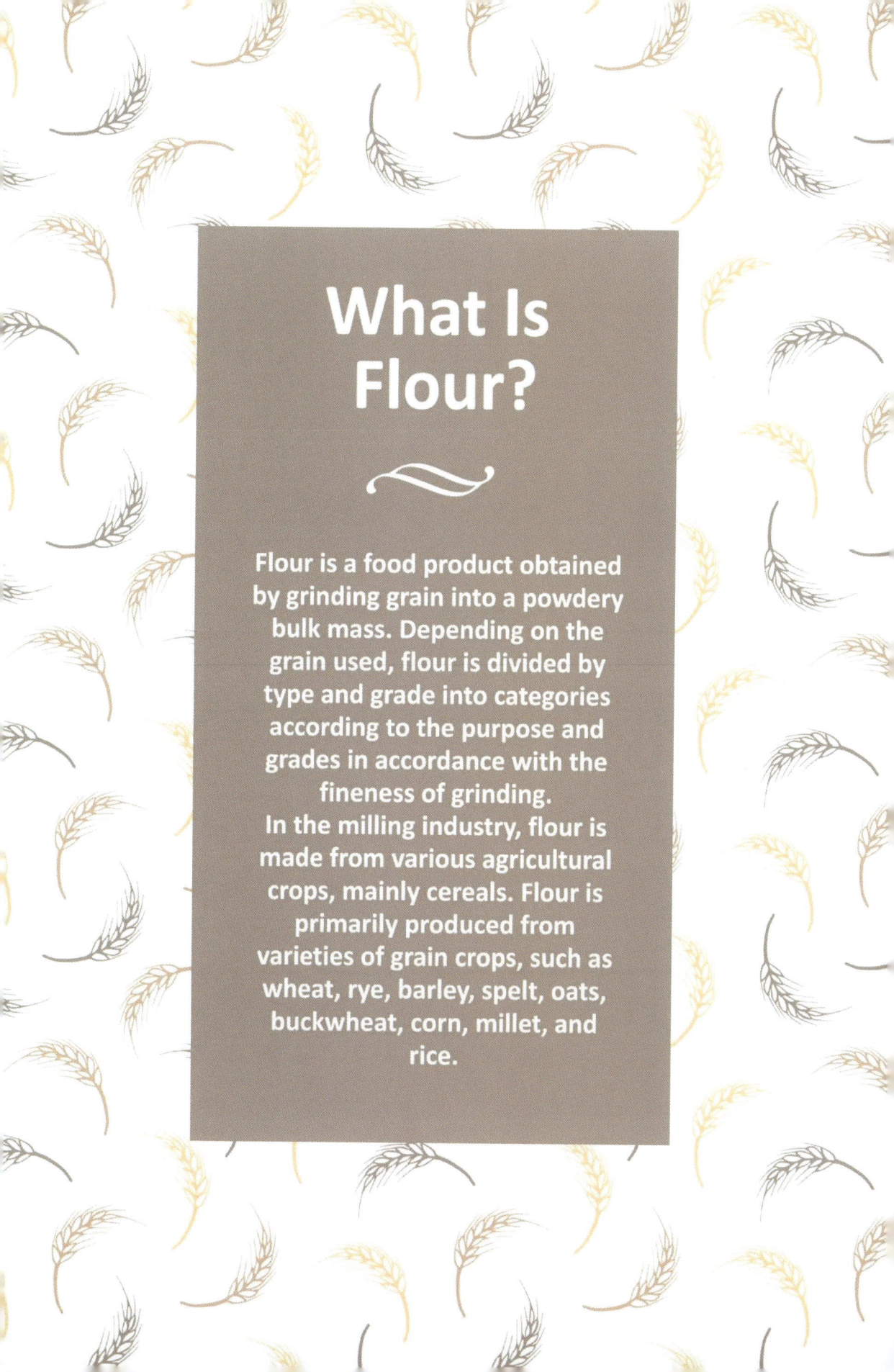

Flour is a food product obtained by grinding grain into a powdery bulk mass. Depending on the grain used, flour is divided by type and grade into categories according to the purpose and grades in accordance with the fineness of grinding.

In the milling industry, flour is made from various agricultural crops, mainly cereals. Flour is primarily produced from varieties of grain crops, such as wheat, rye, barley, spelt, oats, buckwheat, corn, millet, and rice.

Traditional Types of Flour

Most often, wheat and rye flour of various varieties are used for the preparation of bread and bakery products. Other types of flour are used less frequently.

Wheat flour is made from soft wheat varieties. Sometimes, it is allowed to add hard varieties to the mixture, but not more than 20%. Wheat bread flour is divided into grades depending on the size of the grind, gluten content, and whiteness. Moreover, wheat flour contains practically no nutrients.

Fine flour is the most delicate, airy, and suitable flour for baking cake layers, rolls, muffins, and biscuits. It can also be used as a thickener for sauces.

Larger flour is ideal for baking muffins, cakes, and in general, yeast dough. But since it is an uncomfortable dough, it is often not suitable since the grit dough does not rise well and the baked goods quickly turn stale.

Large flour is an excellent choice for those who intend to bake pies, pancakes, rolls, homemade bread, and cookies. This flour is often mixed with rye flour.

The largest dark flour, with a large amount of bran, is most suitable for baking bread. It is tasty and contains a large amount of useful minerals and vitamins.

Rye flour differs from wheat flour in that it has a darker shade and a low gluten content. Therefore, rye bread and rolls retain their freshness for a long time. However, the lack of gluten affects the volume of baked goods; it is not as fluffy, instead it is denser, moist, and has a sour taste. To eliminate this deficiency, it is recommended to mix rye flour with wheat flour. In addition to bread, rye flour makes delicious gingerbread cookies, pancakes, tortillas, muffins, buns, and a fragrant base for kvass.

There are three types of rye flour: fine sifted, medium grinding (includes a certain amount of bran casing), and coarse grinding (whole grain). Whole grain flour is considered the most useful and beneficial flour because it contains the maximum amount of bran, and in terms of the content of proteins, vitamins, useful elements, and amino acids, it is three times higher than wheat flour. Baking from whole grain rye flour stimulates metabolism, lowers cholesterol, and improves heart and stomach function. Rye flour is also used in diets for diabetics.

Non-Traditional Types of Flour

Buckwheat flour is rich in vitamins, minerals, and vegetable protein. It contains amino acids vital for the human body, in addition to natural antioxidants and dietary fiber. At the same time, there are no harmful carbohydrates or gluten in buckwheat flour. Buckwheat flour is an absolutely healthy and useful product. It is versatile, gives baked goods a pleasant chocolate shade, and has an exceptional taste. Almost all the same bakery products can be baked from buckwheat flour as from wheat. The most successful and popular products are from recipes for pancakes, pies, etc. Homemade baked goods made from buckwheat flour are no less tasty than from wheat flour. At the same time, there are much more benefits in buckwheat flour products.

Buckwheat flour can be used to make almost any homemade cake. It is enough to simply replace wheat flour with buckwheat flour in any traditional recipe. Buckwheat flour dough turns out to be extremely tasty, aromatic, and crumbly. The main rule is to add a little more water than usual. Lastly, buckwheat flour is especially luxurious.

Flaxseed flour is a valuable food product obtained from the processing of flaxseeds. The chemical composition of flaxseed flour makes it a very useful product for the body, suitable not only for nutrition, but also as a therapeutic or cosmetic product. The benefits of flaxseed flour are that it contains a lot of plant protein and is rich in amino acids, including essential ones. Flaxseed flour is usually used for baking from unleavened dough, adding it to wheat or corn flour. Moreover, flaxseed meals are low in calories and healthy.

Flaxseed flour is often used for weight loss and in the fight against obesity. However, use flaxseed flour with caution if implementing it as the main component of your diet, since a large amount of this product in the presence of kidney stones and gallbladder can further provoke their movement.

Flaxseed flour does not require prolonged heat treatment, so it can be used to make cereals, sauces, casseroles, and jelly, in addition to filling soups, for mincemeat, and to julienne with. Flaxseed baked goods can be stored for a long time and do not stale.

Oatmeal flour is low in starch and high in plant fiber and fat. Oatmeal contains essential amino acids, as well as many useful vitamins and elements. It also makes pancakes and oatmeal cookies taste and look very good. In addition, oat flour makes baked goods crumblier. Oat flour can replace wheat flour; however, the content of oat flour should not be more than a third of the total amount of flour due to its low amount of gluten. If you need to increase the amount of oat flour in baked goods, then it is recommended to add a little flaxseed flour to the dough, which will act as a binding component and will also increase the biological benefits of the product.

Almond flour is a product obtained from the processing of almonds. This flour is hygroscopic; it is able to absorb and retain moisture well. Thanks to this, baked goods made from almond flour stay fresh longer and do not stale.

The calorie content of almond flour is quite high, and at the same time, it is an unusually valuable product in its chemical composition. Almond flour contains all the valuable components of a fresh nut kernel. Moreover, almond flour products do not lose their beneficial properties even after heat treatment. A particular benefit of almond flour is that it is virtually gluten-free, so it can be used to make a variety of foods and pastries suitable for gluten-sensitive people. It is used to make macaroon cakes, classic marzipan, or desserts with frangipane. It's perfect for making biscuits, various types of dough, nut cream, sweets, and cakes.

Barley flour has practically no taste and smell, is grayish in color, and is sometimes combined with an admixture of bran, which only makes it healthier. Barley flour is a perishable product; it should be stored in a tightly sealed glass or metal container in a cool place. Barley flour contains much more fiber than flours of other grains, so it is often included in diets of people suffering from digestive problems. Tender porridge and crumbly bread are also prepared from barley flour. However, it is worth noting that bread made from barley flour alone quickly becomes stale and crumbles heavily. Therefore, if barley flour is mixed with wheat or rye flour, the bread is excellent. Barley flour is added to dough for tortillas, cookies, pancakes, and fritters. Also, it is sometimes used to thicken soups.

Corn flour contains calcium, magnesium, potassium, iron, and several B vitamins. Furthermore, it is rich in starch and is quite easily absorbed by the body. Fiber is found in corn flour in varying amounts, depending on the purification of flour.

Unlike wheat, corn is a gluten-free crop, which is of importance to certain health advocates. It is used to make cakes, hominy, polenta, pancakes, and other products. The baked goods made primarily from corn flour are very light and crumbly, and are also dietary. Bread products can retain their freshness and aroma for a long time thanks to this particular flour.

Also, based on this product, children's and dietary meals are prepared.

Rice flour is the leader among all grain crops in terms of protein and starch content. The lack of gluten, richness of vitamins, minerals, trace elements, and the beneficial properties of rice flour have turned it into a constant component of children's and dietary meals.

Rice flour can be added to wheat flour to produce crispbreads, rolls, biscuits, and other baked goods that are brittle and porous. If you want the goods to not break or be too dry, you should add more eggs and liquid to the dough and store the products in an airtight container.

Banana flour has become very popular lately. Green banana flour is gluten free, low in fat, moderately rich in protein, and overwhelmingly composed of carbohydrates, primarily starch. However, bananas are not an ordinary starch, but a resistant one, which does not decompose in the human gastrointestinal tract.

Instead, they have an extremely beneficial effect on it. As a gluten-free flour, it is ideal for baked goods, diet desserts, main courses, and soups. The flour is also often used raw, like in sauces, smoothies, and food bars.

Chickpea flour is from chickpeas (lamb peas). This flour is widely used for baking pancakes and tortillas. The products have a delicate nutty smell and taste. In European countries, the ingredient is put into the dough for cakes, pies, and even "macarons." Chickpeas do not contain gluten, so it improves immunity and digestion. It also has a low-calorie content.
Chickpea flour can be used as a substitute for eggs, so meals with chickpea powder can be made completely vegetarian. It is suitable for yeast-free baking; wheat flour must be added to yeast varieties.

Chestnut flour: In certain European countries where edible chestnuts grow, the powder from these fruits is used for baking. Cookies and tortillas are made, in addition to cakes, muffins and bread. For example, in Italy, Tuscan chestnut cake (castagnaccio) is made from chestnut flour. The ingredient is gluten-free and almost completely fat-free, making it great for hypoallergenic and dietary products. Due to the sweet taste of chestnut flour, it requires less sugar in the recipe. When the flour is stored for prolonged periods of time, the sweetness decreases every month, so the fresher the powder, the tastier it is.

Bird cherry flour does not contain gluten, is rich in phytoncides, and has a calorie content that is three times lower than that of wheat flour. It is used for the preparation of bakery and confectionery products, such as cakes, pies, muffins, shortbread cookies, and pastries. This flour gives them a characteristic chocolate color, in addition to the taste and aroma of rum and almonds. It is also used for the preparation of casseroles, fillings for pies and pancakes, and in jelly and pastry cream.

Yeast Leavened Bread-Making Process

Well friends, I hope that now, after reading the previous section, you're able to breathe a sigh of relief, as many things are now clearer to you. Or, hopefully the fog cleared away, and you are full of determination to go further along the path of our exciting adventure to make bread. The most interesting part is ahead of us. We will consider the whole process in detail and I will accompany you at every step. Then, you will definitely be able to keep up and will soon bite into the warm golden-brown crust of your first aromatic bread.

In the process of making bread, we usually need a baking powder to make the bread rise and to get a soft and airy texture. Most loaves use yeast, but some use chemicals, like baking soda or no baking powder at all. The methods used to prepare both types are slightly different.

Now, in general terms, I will introduce you to making yeast bread. I will tell you the general provisions and stages of baking bread so that you have a basic idea of the process, and then when we come to the recipes, you will learn the intricacies of each recipe individually.

Also, I will tell you the step by step preparation of yeast-free bread in another section of this book.

7 Step Yeast Bread Baking Process

1. Yeast Mixture
The first step in making a yeast-leavened bread is preparing the yeast mixture. There are two ways to make this: from prepared commercial yeast and from natural yeast (using a starter). As you already know from above, starter is an analogue of yeast and a sourdough, and it is also the basis for many baked goods.

a. Starter: If you are making a sourdough recipe, you will need to create a starter from a mix of equal parts flour and water. It should be fermented over time to develop the natural form of yeast and bacteria. You will need to create one from scratch, which takes about a week. There is a separate part in the book with more details on preparing and feeding a starter that will be further along. Once you have a mature starter ready at hand, follow the directions in the recipe to create a leaven, and you are good to go.

b. Yeast Mixture: If the recipe calls for commercial yeast, then you will need to add the yeast to warm water or milk, preferably at a temperature of 35°C (95°F) for best results. You may need to add sugar and other ingredients, which I will discuss in the individual recipes. The warm and moist environment will activate the yeast, and you will typically be adding this mixture to your dough in a short amount of time.

2. Weighing and Mixing Ingredients
After preparing your starter or yeast mixture, the next step will involve weighing and mixing your ingredients to create a dough. Make sure your ingredients are at room temperature, and then mix the ingredients thoroughly with the aid of your fingers. Do this until you form a cohesive dough without any visible sign of the

individual components. Some recipes might use different methods to form a dough, but the principle remains the same.

3. Kneading/Folding

Depending upon the hydration of your dough, you will either need to knead or fold your dough. Kneading involves working the dough to develop the gluten in it. Gluten gives the tension necessary for bread to maintain its shape and develop bubbles. For recipes involving sourdough, the high hydration will make the flour challenging to knead, calling for a much gentler method known as folding. The two techniques are discussed in detail below:

a. Kneading: involves you pushing on the center of the dough and then pulling the top part of the stretched dough back over itself in a repetitive manner until the dough becomes tight. You will know when to stop when the dough forms a smooth surface and develops proper tension, which might take several minutes depending upon your speed.

b. Folding: is a gentle process done over time. Wet the fingers of both hands with cool water in the event that the dough sticks to your hands. Then, you will need to pick one end of the dough, stretch it up without letting it tear, and fold it over the center of the dough. Repeat from the other three sides. Cover the dough with a lid and leave for 30 minutes. Repeat the process every thirty minutes until you form a smooth and tight dough.

4. Bulk Fermentation

After combining the starter culture with the dough, the bulk fermentation will occur. This is a process in which the yeast breaks down the sugars in the dough and converts it into carbon dioxide gas, which is also responsible for the bubbly and airy texture of the bread. The time for the ferment again depends on the recipe and will be discussed in more detail later.

5. Shaping (molding)

After the bulk ferment, you will notice that your dough looks nothing like the final bread should look. Here is where shaping comes into play. The essence of molding is to give the dough its final shape, and the baker's task is to do it so that the dough keeps its form, but at the same time remains soft on the inside and well stretched and strong on the outside. Shaping will also allow you to form your dough into popular forms, like baguettes and rolls. I will describe shaping in more detail in each recipe. After shaping, you will typically place your dough in a loaf pan or banneton to proof.

6. Proofing

When we were kneading the dough to give the test elasticity to the form, most of the gas came out of it. So, we need to continue the fermentation process in order to get an attractive curvaceous form. During proofing, the amount of gas in the dough rises rapidly and reaches the desired level. That allows your bread to rise before baking. Proofing is necessary for developing a light and fluffy bread. The time taken for proofing is important. However, you might wonder how to know that the workpiece has come up and also, if it's time to bake. When you are beginner, look at the speed of levelling the dough after finger pressing. If the dough levels out quickly, then the dough is not ready yet. If it levels out slowly or there is a noticeable trace, then you can bake. Lastly, if a trace remains for a long time, you either pressed too hard or the dough had too much time waiting. But, in the process, learn to gain experience and observe the state of the test within. You should grow to learn the precise moment when the dough is fluffy, airy, and bubbly, which means that the dough is ready for baking.

What else affects the proofing speed?

Temperature in general
The warmer the room, the faster the proofing process. But at the same time, it is worth considering the temperature of the dough. If it is initially low (all the ingredients were cold; the sourdough and water were from the refrigerator), then the proofing may be delayed since the dough will take additional time to warm up and begin to ferment. At the same time, the cooler it is in the room and the lower the temperature of the dough, the longer it will take to mature.

Time
If your dough rose well during the fermentation stage, then the proofing will be rapid and last at least half the length of the fermentation stage. If the dough came up poorly during fermentation, then the proofing will be delayed.

Test composition
The coarser the flour in the dough, whether it be wheat or rye, the faster it will ferment. In addition, the presence of whole grain flour leads to the fastest proofing of the various flours. This is because whole-grain flour is rich in enzymes, and because of which, the dough ferments faster, quickly decays, spreads, and sticks. Dough

made from white flour or with minor additions of whole grain flour behaves more stable, strains, and spreads much more slowly.

Forming density

The speed of proofing the workpiece depends on how much and how tight you form your workpiece during molding. The more the dough is tightened, the more tense its gluten is and the longer it takes to proof.

7. Baking

Baking is the final step in the making of your bread and is also one of the most critical steps. As your bread bakes, the dough's top layer forms a crust that will brown over time. In order for the bread to develop and rise in the oven gradually, steam must be introduced into the oven. You can provide the steam by placing an ovenproof dish filled with ice cubes when you add your bread. The temperature at which your bread bakes is also essential and will vary between recipes, but the final result must be a beautiful golden-brown crust with a light and fluffy interior. After baking, make sure to cool your bread for an hour or until it reaches room temperature.

What You Should Know About a Starter

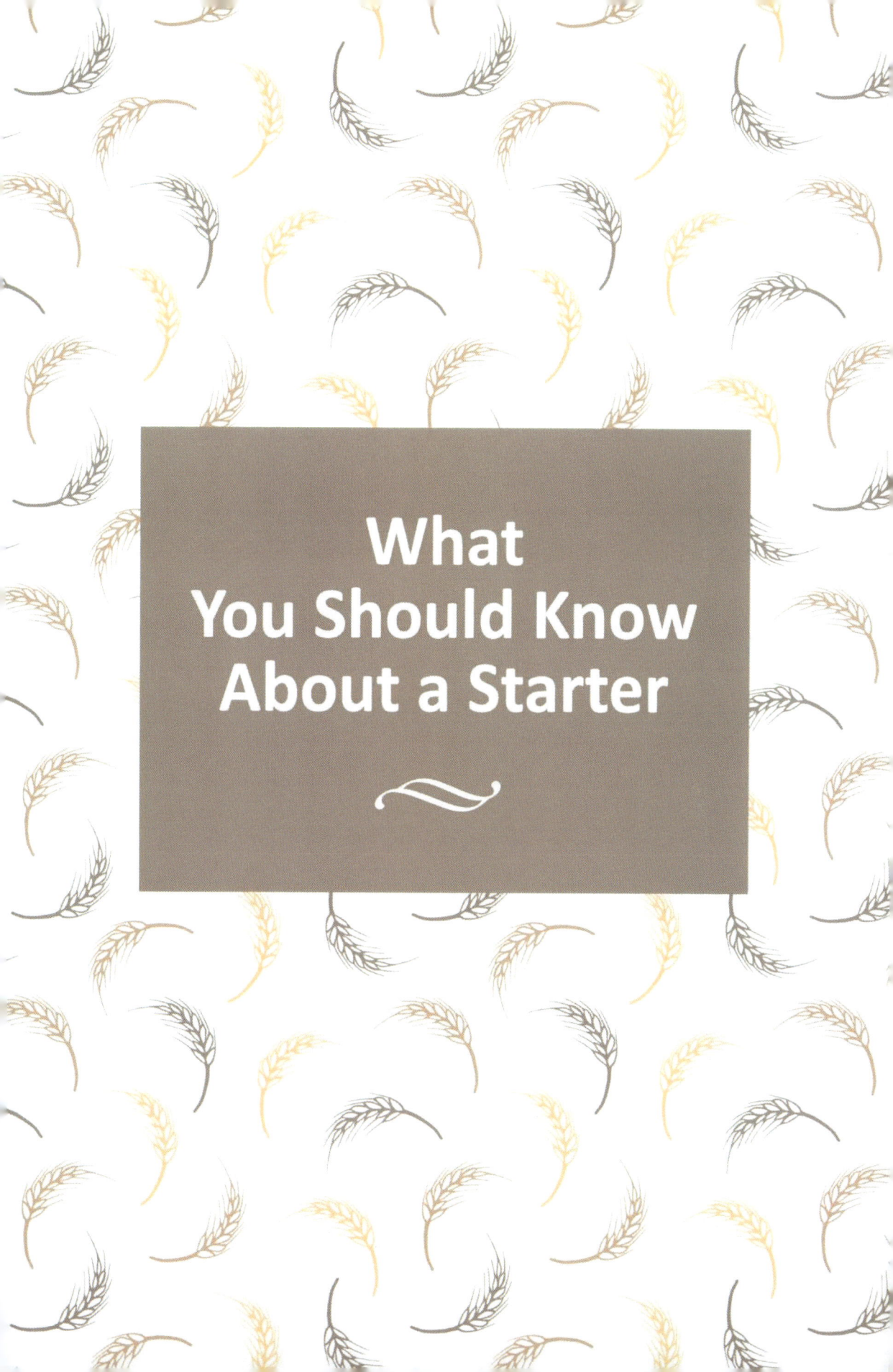

To make your sourdough loaf, you will need a sourdough starter. A sourdough starter is essentially a sour dough where wild yeast (which makes bread rise) and lactic acid bacteria live. Lactic acid bacteria feed on the waste products of the yeast and create an acidic environment in which this yeast lives well but various fungi, mold, and other "bad" bacteria do not survive. Therefore, we can say that they exist on mutually beneficial terms. Both are contained in air, water, and flour, and thus get into the starter. To separate these, we only need flour and water, and well, patience.

To get you started with your very own sourdough starter, I have written down a 7-day schedule to begin the process that you must follow. To create and maintain your starter, you will need a glass jar with a capacity of at least 500ml, a kitchen weighing scale, the required amounts of flour and filtered water, and a spatula that fits into your jar for mixing. Also, be sure to use organic, non-chlorinated flour and water for your starter. The water *must* be non-chlorinated. If bleach is added to your tap water to neutralize microorganisms, then it is not suitable for us, because our beneficial starter microorganisms will also suffer from it. If there is no other alternative, then boiled tap water can be used.

The easiest way to get a sourdough starter from rye flour is through the use of whole grain. This is because the microorganisms that participate in fermentation and the enzymes that activate various processes in it live precisely in the parts of the grain that are removed during the production of refined flour. However, whole grain flour is very different from refined flour. Using whole grain flour may sometimes not go well and you will have to try another manufacturer's flour. This flour must also be sifted. When sifting, we saturate the flour with oxygen. Also, the flour should be fresh. It is preferrable that no more than two months have passed from the date of production. If bran remains in the sieve when sifting flour, add it to the sourdough starter.

When the flour is mixed with water and placed in a jar, we will have to arm ourselves with a room thermometer and find a suitable place for the starter. Fermented yeast develops well at temperatures above 25 degrees Celsius on average. But lactic acid bacteria, which also develops in the starter and helps it overcome pathogenic bacteria, like a hot environment with a temperature over 30°. So, it is best to put the jar in a place with temperature around 24-26°; this temperature is equally comfortable for yeast and lactic acid bacteria. The lower limit is 23 degrees; at temperatures less than 22 degrees, both the bacteria and yeast will develop slowly, which means that it will be more difficult to overcome putrefactive fermentation, which is when pathogenic bacteria develop. Also, the process of forming the starter microflora will be difficult and long.

You should not put the starter:
- ✓ on the battery; it warms up unevenly and too much
- ✓ in the oven; it's hot, stuffy, and dry
- ✓ in a tightly closed cabinet; there may be little oxygen and it is dry
- ✓ covered with several towels; there is no oxygen access
- ✓ wrapped in a blanket; it still won't warm itself, because, unlike a person, it doesn't generate heat
- ✓ in a place where it will be strongly exposed to the sun; this is a stress factor for microorganisms

If the room is cool, you can try to look for a warm place somewhere closer to the ceiling (on a hanging cabinet, for example), or put it in a water bath (not in hot water, of course), or near a battery, or, if there are no options at all, on the battery itself, but on a towel folded several times but while making sure that the starter does not dry out.

So, let's go!

How to Grow a Starter in 6 Days

Day 1
Required:
- 100 ml of water at room temperature
- 100 ml whole grain rye flour
- clean glass liter jar
- sieve

1. Sift about 100 ml of flour (half a glass).

2. Pour 100 ml of water into a jar and add the sifted flour along with the bran remaining in the sieve. Do this in such an amount that you reach a consistency of a thin (on the first day, it should be thin so that in conditions of high humidity, all bacteria and enzymes understand that it is time to wake up and get to work).

3. It makes no sense to indicate the exact amount of flour to a gram since all flour is different, even whole grain, and it will also take slightly different amounts of water. Moreover, different types of flour have different density, which means the volume is not an exact parameter. You should focus on consistency. Mix.

4. Close the jar with double gauze under an elastic band, with a paper napkin, or with a cloth and put in a moderately warm place with a temperature of 24-28 degrees.

5. The temperature regime is very important; often the reason for deviations from the normal course of the formation of starter microflora is because of a temperature too low or too high (like when the starter was placed on a battery, carefully wrapped in a blanket).

6. You do not need to stir the starter culture during infusion!

Day 2

After checking the starter, we should find:
- ✓ bubbles and something like foam on the surface (this may not always be the case)
- ✓ the starter smells unpleasant
- ✓ the starter has more liquid than when we left it

The starter may rise on the first and second days or may not rise at all; it all depends on what microorganisms are in it. Both are within the normal range; neither one nor the other is a sign of her readiness. The fact is that in the first days of fermentation, all types of microorganisms that were in the flour multiply in it, and can possibly get into it from the water, air, or from our hands. Among them are pathogenic microorganisms, some of which may be active gas formers, hence the rise of the starter culture at this stage.

At this stage, a rotten smell may occur in the starter. But together with the pathogenic ferment, the useful ferment microflora we need develops; firstly, lactic acid bacteria, and secondly, yeast. Lactic acid bacteria release organic acids that have antibacterial effects, such as acetic acid and other antimicrobial and antifungal agents. These substances accumulate in the starter and gradually make the vital activity of harmful microorganisms impossible.

The following course of the process is also normal: when the starter rises on the first or second day, then stops rising, and then, after the unpleasant smell changes to a pleasant one (i.e. on the 4th day approximately), it begins to rise again. It is also normal when the starter initially, at the stage of putrefactive fermentation, does not rise until after three days. A sign of the readiness of the starter is its rise in the stage of lactic acid fermentation, when all the pathogenic microbes have already died starting from about the fourth day.

1. Refill the jar with 100 ml of room temperature water.
2. Sift flour through a sieve.
3. Pour the sifted flour together with the bran left over during sifting into the jar so that the consistency of a thick cream is obtained. From this day on and on the following days, the mixture should have the consistency of thick cream or yogurt.
4. Mix.
5. Cover with a gauze or napkin.
6. Put it in a warm place with a temperature of 24-28°.

Day 3

Two days have passed. The smell is still unpleasant, and there are small bubbles on the surface. Again, add 100 ml of water and 100 ml of sifted flour with bran until the starter reaches the consistency of thick sour cream. Stir, cover with gauze, and put in a place with a temperature of about 24-26°.

Day 4

Three days have passed. The smell is much better. This means that lactic acid fermentation has won over putrefactive. If this does not happen, the starter should be fed again according to the scheme of the previous day. If the smell improves, the starter should be separated. Put half of the starter culture in a clean jar, add an equal amount of water to the volume of the starter culture, stir, then add sifted flour with bran to reach the usual consistency of thick sour cream, stir again, cover with gauze, put in a warm place, and wait for it to rise. Discard any remaining starter.

Remove half of the starter culture so that the microorganisms receive enough feeding. If at this stage you feed the starter culture with a smaller amount of nutrient mixture than in a 1:1 ratio, there will be insufficient nutrition for microorganisms. If you feed the starter in the specified proportion without dividing it, then the starter will greatly increase and will surely escape from the jar.

Day 5

The fifth feeding occurs; the age of the starter is four days.

Over the past day, the starter should have acquired an important skill: it should begin to "walk or move," that is, rise and fall.

In addition, the starter culture should have a pleasant smell (something like berry-wine-herbal-fermented milk), bubble vigorously, and have increased in volume by 2-2.5 times. When feeding, divide it again, transplant half of it into a clean jar (discard the remaining half), pour water in the same volume equal to the volume of the starter, and add the sifted flour, then return the bran remaining in the sieve there. There should be a consistency of thick sour cream, then cover it and put in the usual place.

Day 6
Five days have passed. If the starter has risen and gone down, we can say that it is basically ready.

Signs of a mature leaven:
- ✓ the smell is pleasant
- ✓ the taste is very sour
- ✓ it is filled with gas bubbles throughout the entire volume (when the starter is standing for a long time, the gas bubbles

may no longer be visible on the surface; that does not matter, for the main thing is that when feeding, they should appear again)
- ✓ the ability to significantly increase in volume (two times)

In general, even at this stage, you can try to bake bread.
But the starter is still young, weak, and in order to consolidate the properties of the starter and its "strength," I recommend feeding it 2-3 more times.
1st time - according to the scheme of Day 5 (that is, starter and water in equal proportions 1:1).
2nd and 3rd times - if the starter already copes with this amount of feeding faster than in a day, then you can feed it according to the proportions of a starter: water = 1:2 and 1:3. This means putting half of the starter culture in a clean jar, adding two (or three) times more water, and adding flour to the usual consistency of thick sour cream, then stirring and putting it aside to infuse.
In other words, if a young sourdough eats a feed in a volume equal to itself per day, then feed it 1:1. When she begins to cope with this amount of food in half a day, then give her twice the amount of food (when feeding, pour in two times more water than the starter).
Ideally, you can gradually bring these proportions to 1:4 - 1:5.

Storage of Starter Culture

At a temperatures less than 10 degrees, the metabolism of lactic acid bacteria and yeast will slow down to one degree or another, resulting in a violation of the quantitative relationships between these types of microorganisms. And, if the lactic acid bacteria are weakened, the fermentation processes in the dough will occur differently, and the bread will not have its usual benefits. In addition, the starter culture will become less protected, acquire an unpleasant odor, change color, and become vulnerable to mold. If yeast is suppressed, this will not fail to negatively affect the lifting force of the starter.

Therefore, the starter culture should be stored at a temperature of around 10-14 degrees!

Accordingly, if she lives in the refrigerator, there should be a slight increase in temperature to the specified value using a temperature switch.

Or, find another place in the house, armed with a thermometer.

Another option is to leave the starter at the temperatures available (20-35°, depending on the season) and feed it as soon as it needs it (for example, if it stratifies and smells sad). But this option is tough enough for the hostess; in the heat, the starter may require feeding up to twice a day.

Thus, the place where the starter culture is stored should be cool and protected from direct sunlight, as this is a stress factor for microorganisms and a source of mold.

How to Feed a Starter

Ideally, you should feed the rye starter once a day if you keep it at room temperature. You need to feed in such proportions that its rise and subsidence would occur just as long as it takes between feeding (usually 1:4 is enough for a day).

But this is not always convenient and possible for the hostess, so you can keep the sourdough in the refrigerator. It should be fed at least once every 5-7 days (maximum 10) if bread is not baked. If bread *is* baked, the sourdough feeding should be timed to prepare the starter for the dough.

With prophylactic feeding, you should:
- ✓ retrieve the starter culture a few hours before feeding to warm up to room temperature;
- ✓ pour water at room temperature into a clean jar in a volume 4-5 times greater than the volume of the transplanted amount of the starter culture (for example, 200 ml of water for 40 ml (2 tablespoons) of the starter culture),
- ✓ add starter culture (a selected amount; for example, 2 tablespoons),
- ✓ stir,
- ✓ add sifted whole grain flour with bran-seeded (what remains in the sieve) until the consistency of thick sour cream is attained, mix;
- ✓ wait until the sourdough rises to a peak, the minimum settles to half and the maximum settles completely to the initial level; then, let it stand for another 4-8 hours until the smell of a mature sourdough (and a very sour taste) is acquired; if the sourdough is exposed to the cold earlier, not all pathogenic organisms introduced with a new portion of flour will be suppressed since the sourdough will not have time to gain the required acidity (which is its main defense);
- ✓ put away in the chosen cool storage area.

How to Refresh a Sourdough Before Using it to Make Bread

In whatever conditions the starter culture is stored, if more than two days have passed since feeding, the microbiological composition and working qualities of the starter culture will still change. After all, the quantitative ratios of microorganisms and their state will no longer correspond to the original ones. So, we will take out a completely different sourdough than the one that we put in the refrigerator, and it will no longer be quite suitable for making bread. This can be easily seen by comparing the refreshed active starter culture with the starter culture after storage. The starter from the refrigerator will be a sluggish liquid with an unpleasant odor (most often acetic and bitter). It will be possibly stratified and possibly moldy, and in a few words, weak and inoperative. The difference will be seen both in the way the dough raises and in the taste of the bread. The dough will fit sluggishly, the crumb structure will be shapeless and poorly loosened, and the taste will be poor, if not unpleasant. Also, the bread will not have the expected beneficial effect on the body either.

On the other hand, the rejuvenated sourdough will smell good, have a light, bubble-filled structure, and perform its role beautifully and energetically — fermenting and loosening the dough. When we fed the starter before the dough, we filled it with young microorganisms and returned their balance to the original one. Both yeast and, most importantly, lactic acid bacteria after feeding are vigorous and ready to work.

Rejuvenation, in fact, is the same as the usual prophylactic feeding, only it is performed in a certain time frame — about a day before the preparation of the dough-shutter. I will say it again: if the starter has been in the refrigerator for more than two days, it is imperative to feed it before making bread.

Accordingly, the scheme here is exactly the same, but nonetheless, I will describe it again:
- ✓ take the starter culture out of the refrigerator and let it warm up to room temperature for several hours,
- ✓ pour 100 to 200 ml of water into a clean jar (depending on how much starter you need for bread),
- ✓ put 1-2 tablespoons of warmed starter in the jar,
- ✓ add whole grain sifted rye flour together with bran-sowing until the consistency of thick sour cream is reached.

The mixture should rise, settle, and infuse, ultimately acquiring a pleasant smell of working sourdough. After that, you can prepare dough with the starter as the basis.
Part of the rejuvenated sourdough is taken for making the dough, the rest is put into the refrigerator for storage. The old starter from which you took these two spoons should not be stored. It would not make sense to keep it because it has ceased to work.

6 Starter Problems and Solutions

Problem one: Sourdough stands and stands, but there are no signs of fermentation (bubbles and increase in volume).

Option 1: It's a matter of temperature. Optimal temperature for starter culture is 24-27 degrees. The lower limit is 23 degrees; at a temperatures less than 22 degrees, yeast will develop slowly, which means that the process of forming the starter microflora will be difficult and long.

Option 2: It's about consistency. The sourdough should be mixed exactly like thick sour cream. If it is mixed to liquid, like kefir, then it will exfoliate and starve. If it is thick, like cottage cheese, then it will be too difficult for her to ferment at room temperature and gain acidity. Moreover, it is difficult to overcome pathogenic microflora and it is difficult to start moving.

Option 3: It's about flour. Freshness is the main factor. Flour must be fresh with no more than two months from the date of issue.
Another factor is the type of flour. If the flour is peeled, and not whole grain, problems are more likely. This is because the microorganisms involved in fermentation and the enzymes that activate it that live in the parts of the grain that are removed during the production of peeled and sown flour.
Another factor is the size of the grind. It is difficult to remove the sourdough with coarse flour.
And finally, it can just be the flour. All flour is different. It might be worth trying another manufacturer's flour.

Option 4: It's about water. It is unlikely that someone will take water from the tap because there may be chlorine in the water, which is added precisely because of its antibacterial effect. But in the same way, beneficial fermenting microorganisms will suffer from it.
Purchased bottled water or spring water can also cause problems. If you strictly follow the recipe, but there is no effect, and you are sure of the quality of the flour, try another brand of bottled water.

The springs, unfortunately, in our time are also not always as clean as they should be. So, you can try to boil the spring water, and if this does not work, then, again, try another brand of bottled water.

Option 5: Part of the issue may be air access. Lactic acid bacteria can grow without air access. However, yeast is fine to breathe. Only when breathing (with air access) does it emit carbon dioxide, and the bubbles that we see in the test are carbon dioxide. Close the starter jar with a double layer of cheesecloth, a cloth not a plastic lid, and remember to sift through the flour.

Option 6: Signs of fermentation are simply not visible when viewed from above (this happens when using coarse flour). Look from the side; perhaps the mass of starter dough is already full of the cherished bubbles.

Problem two: The starter is stratified.

Sourdough stratification is common and is caused in most cases by an overly liquid consistency. The lowest acceptable density of the sourdough is the equality of the volumes of water and flour in its composition, which should give it a cream-like consistency. The consistency can be denser, but for such a starter, it is important to be warm, otherwise it will be difficult for it to "leaven." In general, high humidity is preferable for enzymes because it is easier for them to work in a creamy consistency. A measuring tool is very important here: too liquid - it stratifies and will starve and suffer, too thick - it will swing for a long time at room temperature during fermentation.

Layering also occurs when the liquid sourdough is warm. Therefore, a sourdough of the consistency of yogurt means an almost 100% chance of stratification in the morning.

Problem three: Sourdough rose in the first two days, then stopped.

The starter may rise on the first and second days or may not rise at all. It all depends on what microorganisms are in it. Both are within the normal range; neither one nor the other is a sign of her readiness. The fact is that in the first days of fermentation, all types of microorganisms that were in the flour multiply in it and can possibly get into it from water, air, or from our hands. Some of them may turn out to be active gas formers, hence the rise of the starter culture at the initial stage of hatching.

However, in accordance with the pathogenic ferment, the useful ferment microflora that we need develops - first, lactic acid bacteria, and secondly, yeast (only acid-resistant types of yeast can take root in rye ferment). Lactic acid bacteria secrete organic acids with antibacterial action (acetic, for example) and other antimicrobial and antifungal substances; these substances accumulate in the starter and gradually make the vital activity of harmful microorganisms impossible, since under conditions of such high acidity, almost nothing can survive. So, as the acidity increases, only the yeast that we need remains in the starter. Accordingly, the rise that occurs *after* the change of an unpleasant smell to a pleasant one, that is, after the formation of lactic acid fermentation for three days, is a legitimate and correct rise. It is caused by the right microorganisms, and therefore indicates that the process of maturation of the sourdough is proceeding successfully and is approaching its completion.

Thus, the following course of the process is also normal: the starter rises on the first or second day, stops rising, and then, after the unpleasant smell changes to a pleasant one (on the 4th day approximately), it begins to rise again. In this case, most likely, it first rose from harmful bacteria and then from the correct ones.

Another scenario, also normal, is when the starter does not initially rise and begins to smell like rot, then begins to rise only after three days.

Important: Three signs of readiness, efficiency, and a healthy rye sourdough are:
- ✓ the ability to increase two times
- ✓ a pleasant smell (without yeast, alcohol, acetone, or putrefactive notes)
- ✓ a very sour taste (close to the taste of lemon juice).

Problem four: The starter smells bad for two days.

This is completely normal! In the first days of breeding the starter, all types of microorganisms multiply in it, which could get into it from the flour, water, air, and from our hands. Among them are putrefactive, pathogenic microorganisms, and it is clear that the products of their vital activity can have a very far from pleasant smell. Therefore, this phase is called the phase of putrefactive fermentation. After a while, the acidic environment will kill them, and we will only have bacteria useful for the fermentation of bread.

Problem five: White bloom on sourdough.

This is definitely a deviation from the norm. Either this is evidence of excessive activity of the yeast living in the starter, or evidence of the ingress and reproduction of an extraneous fungus or bacteria. In both cases, this means that the natural defense mechanisms of the starter culture do not work. This means the lactic acid bacteria are either deprived of the opportunity to exercise their protective qualities, are suppressed, or there are too few of them, and, accordingly, little acid is released to kill pathogenic organisms. This is a signal that the wrong feeding or storage mode has been selected. Insufficiently thick mix often contributes to this. In addition, it can be because of the quality of the flour and water.

Make sure the flour is fresh and of good quality. Then, try feeding the starter culture in such a way that the bacteria can work at full strength: remove the plaque and the layer under it, transfer 50 ml of the starter culture to a clean jar, add 100 ml of water, add flour to reach the consistency of a thick cream (when the jar is tilted, the mixture moves, but slowly), let the sourdough rise, fall, and then always let it stand for 6-8 hours after it settles. Do this for 3-4 days. If the rise takes place quickly, then increase the amount of feeding by 50 ml of starter culture and 200 ml of water. If the plaque does not go away, remove a new starter, as it is better with new flour.

Important: Any color other than white that looks like a mold means the starter must be recovered!

Problem six: Dry sourdough crust.

If the starter culture is covered with a dense crust when feeding, it should be placed as far away from the battery and other sources of dry air as possible. It should also be covered with something denser than it was covered with before, but also breathable, like a damp cloth.

Cure a Starter

The most important tool in ferment diagnostics is our nose. Remember how the starter smells in its working, active state. Take this smell as the norm and track any deviations from it.
The main causes of problems with starter culture are non-compliance with storage conditions and insufficient nutrition (irregular feeding). The main treatment is proper nutrition: one or more preventive feeding.

Signs that the starter is hungry, but, in general, nothing particularly terrible has happened to it, are:
- ✓ alcohol smell
- ✓ not a pungent vinegar smell
- ✓ hard crust, but when removed, an acceptable smell (remove the crust and discard)
- ✓ the leaven has exfoliated and there is transparent water on top (drain the liquid, and when feeding, make sure that the consistency of the leaven is not too liquid).

In these cases, you just need to feed the starter culture according to the preventive feeding scheme once or twice for peace of mind.

Signs that something is wrong with the starter, but the situation can be corrected by timely feeding and careful care:
- ✓ not a strong yeast smell
- ✓ thin white bloom (remove and discard, and when feeding, make sure that the consistency is not liquid)
- ✓ unpleasant odor
- ✓ hard crust, but when removed, a rancid odor (remove the crust and discard)
- ✓ the leaven has stratified, and there is black water on top (drain the liquid, make sure that the consistency is not liquid when feeding)
- ✓ sharp acetone, "varnish-colored" smell.

All of these are signs of a weakening starter and, possibly, the development of foreign species of microorganisms in it (which becomes possible precisely because of the weakening of its protective properties). The problem goes away with the observance of the storage regime and proper nutrition. Treatment here is abundant, including regular feeding according to a preventive scheme for several days. Be sure to put the starter culture in a clean jar! Let me remind you that the starter should rise and settle, and only then should receive a new portion of the nutrient mixture.

Signs that something is wrong with the starter, but correcting this is generally a thankless task and it is better to bring out a new starter:
- ✓ a strong yeast odor and the appearance of plaque in the form of yeast spores
- ✓ the appearance of frank mold (green and black)

- ✓ the leaven has exfoliated and there is a bloom or hard crust on top, then when removed, there is black water and a sharp unpleasant smell

But this can happen only if the elementary rules for caring for the starter were not followed, and most importantly, if the leaven was starving for a very long time.

Yeast Bread Recipes

～

Now that you have everything you need, including a ready-made starter, we can get down to the fun part: mixing all the ingredients according to the recipes and getting our desired bread! In this book, I will give you the simplest bread options so you can start with them, understand the process, have your first experience, follow the instructions clearly, and in the future, be able to make more complex recipes and experiments in baking bread.

Sourdough Loaf Recipe

Ingredients:

Levain:
- **30 grams of Mature Starter:** A mature starter is what you have after following the starter schedule for seven days. Make sure that you have fed the starter the day before, and you are good to go.
- **30 grams of All-Purpose flour:** All-purpose flour is a type of wheat flour where the bran of the wheat grain is absent. For the best results, make sure the flour you use is unbleached.
- **30 grams of Whole Wheat flour:** Whole wheat flour is a flour that consists of the entire wheat kernel.
- **60 grams of Water:** Make sure to use filtered water at room temperature.

Dough:
- **150 grams of the Levain**
- **750 grams of Bread Flour:** Bread flour is very similar to all-purpose flour but has a higher gluten content of 11-15%. Also, make sure that the flour is unbleached.
- **150 grams of Whole Wheat Flour**
- **100 grams of Rye Flour:** As the name suggests, rye flour is the flour made from rye berries and is similar to wheat flour in regard to consistency.
- **770 grams of Water:** Make sure to use filtered water.
- **20 grams of Salt:** Use a non-iodized salt, like sea salt, and make sure it has fine grains.

Steps:

1. Begin by weighing the contents of the levain. Pick a clean mason jar that has a capacity of at least 500ml. A good practice is placing the jar on top of your weighing scale and using the tare option to set the weight to zero. Start with your mature starter, ensuring that it has risen at least by double and that the surface is bubbly and concave. Add this to the jar and proceed by adding the required amounts of flour and water. Using a spatula, combine the mixture thoroughly until no bits of flour are visible. Then, cover the jar with a loose-fitting lid and place it in an environment with a consistent temperature for about 5-6 hours.

2. Now, we will begin the autolyze. One and a half hours before your starter is ready, it is time to mix the ingredients for your dough. Take a large mixing bowl and place it on your weighing scale, using the tare button to set the scale to zero. Add the three flours one by one, keeping in mind to check the correct weight each time. After adding your flour, mix the ingredients thoroughly with your dry, bare hands.

3. Measure the 770 grams of water and separate 50g from it to use later. Check the temperature of the remaining 720 grams of water and make sure it's between 27-29°C (80-85°F), heating if necessary. Add the water to your mixing bowl and use your hands to form a cohesive mixture leaving behind no dry bits of dough. If the dough sticks to your hands, use a bench scraper to get it off. Cover it with a damp kitchen towel or shrink wrap and leave it for the remainder of the time needed for your levain to rise, which is about an hour.

4. After your levain and dough mixture have rested, you will need to add the starter, salt, and remaining water to the dough mixture. The dough mixture must be firm. If you notice it is too sticky or fluid, add only a splash from the 50g of water with the help of your hands. Pour the starter, salt, and water, in that order, over the dough mixture and poke holes through the dough with all your fingers and mix it thoroughly. You can also pick up the dough from one side and slap it down in the bowl in a continuous process to incorporate it further.

5. Then, let the dough rest, covered, for 4-5 hours for the bulk ferment. During this time, you will need to perform four stretches and folds spaced 30 minutes apart. I have already mentioned the process in the previous section, so give it a read. After the fourth fold, let the dough rest for the remainder of the ferment. Make sure the environment you rest your dough is warm and not in direct contact with sunlight.

6. After the bulk ferment, you will notice that your dough will have risen by about 50-80% and have a bubbly texture. You must see a considerable rise, otherwise, let it ferment for another hour and check again later. Now, flour a clean and dry surface like your kitchen top and lightly dump the dough onto the surface, being careful not to remove the built-up gas inside.

7. Flour a thin line on the surface of your dough to divide it into two parts and, with the help of a bench scraper, cut through the dough, dividing it into two sections. Lightly flour your hands and form half of the dough into a tight ball by rotating it towards you with the help of the scraper. Repeat for the other half. Let this bench rest uncovered for 25 minutes.

8. After the bench rest, lightly flour the surface of your dough and using a bench scraper, loosen the bottom and flip it upside down. Now, flour your fingers and pick the end of the dough nearest to you, then gently fold it towards the center of the dough. Then, take the left side of your dough, stretch it, and fold it about two-thirds of the way to the right. Now, pull and fold the right side entirely over the left. After this, stretch the farthest end of the dough and pull it all the way back, forming it into a round boule. Again, rotate the boule with the help of your bench scraper for a couple of times.

9. Generously flour the surface of your banneton with some rice flour and using the scraper, lift the boule into the banneton. If you don't have a banneton, use a round bowl with a clean towel on the inside and follow the same process for placing the boule inside. Repeat the process with the other boule, placing it in a separate bowl or banneton.

10. Put each banneton or bowl in a puffed-up airtight plastic or zip-lock bag and place it in the fridge for 14-16 hours to proof. To check if your dough has properly proofed, poke the surface with your finger. If it bounces back, leaving a small dent on the surface, it has proved correct. If it bounces back without leaving a dent, then prove it for another hour or more and repeat.

11. Take your banneton or bowl from the fridge and flour the surface of the dough. Take your Dutch oven or baking tray and place it in your oven. If you are using a tray, also put an ovenproof bowl lined with foil in your oven. Set the temperature to 260°C (500°F) and preheat the oven for one hour. Take the Dutch oven or baking tray out of the oven and lightly flour its surface. Take your container and invert the dough into the tray or Dutch oven, then take a sharp knife or razor and gently score a large square on the surface of your dough.

12. Place the dough in the oven. If you are using a Dutch oven, place the lid on, and if you are using a baking tray, fill the foil-lined bowl with roughly 10-15 ice cubes and bake for 20 minutes at 260°C (500°F). After the 20 minutes, remove the lid from your Dutch oven or remove the bowl with the ice cubes from the oven and reduce the temperature. Then, cook at 232°C (450°F) for another 20 minutes until the top of the bread is a beautiful golden brown and a thermometer placed inside the loaf registers at 98°C (208°F).

13. Take your loaf out of the oven and immediately repeat the process for the other loaf. Place the finished loaf on a wire rack and let it cool for an hour or until it reaches room temperature. After this, you can slice the bread with a serrated knife and enjoy your sourdough loaf.

Milk Bread Roll Recipe

Ingredients:

Tangzhong:
- **60 grams of Whole Milk:** Make sure the container clearly states whole milk.
- **40 grams of Bread Flour:** Bread flour is very similar to all-purpose flour but has a higher gluten content of 11-15%. Also, make sure that the flour is unbleached.

Dough:
- **300 grams of Bread Flour**
- **2 Teaspoons of Active Dried Yeast:** You can also use instant yeast, but make sure that the yeast you are using is at room temperature and is not older than three months.
- **120 grams of Whole Milk**
- **1 Teaspoon of Fine Salt:** Use natural sea-salt that is not iodized for the best results.
- **50 grams of Granulated Sugar:** You can determine if the sugar is granulated if it has a crystalline form.
- **1 Egg:** Make sure your egg is at room temperature.
- **56 grams of Unsalted Butter:** Keep the butter out and let it soften.

Eggwash:
- **1 Egg:**
- **2 Tablespoons of Milk**

Steps:

1. A tangzhong is what gives milk bread its extremely fluffy texture. To prepare it, you will need to add the tangzhong ingredients to a cold saucepan or pot, place it on your stove, turn it to medium, and stir with a whisk continuously until it forms a thick paste, similar to glue, which can take up to two minutes. Remove from the heat and let it cool down to room temperature.

2. While that cools, warm the milk for your dough to a temperature of around 35°C (98°F), add the yeast and sugar, gently stir, and then set it aside to activate for about 10 minutes or until it becomes bubbly and foamy.

3. Once the tangzhong has cooled and the yeast bloomed, beat your room temperature egg thoroughly until mixed and add it along with the yeast mixture to a mixing bowl. Add the tangzhong, the remainder of your flour and the salt, and mix it with your hands until it forms a shaggy dough, making sure no dry bits of flour are left. Lightly flour a work surface like your kitchen countertop and dump your flour onto the surface.

4. Start kneading the dough with your hands, making sure to work it thoroughly until the dough becomes smooth and tight. You will know when to stop when the dough becomes tight and can maintain its round shape without collapsing. Also, the dough will be a lot less sticky than it initially was. Do not stop kneading until you have reached this stage. Let the dough rest for a minute or two.

5. Now, divide your butter into several cubes and place them on the surface of your dough. Fold the dough over so that the butter is incorporated and begin kneading again. You will notice that the butter has made the dough a little oily and tough to work with but nonetheless, continue kneading for 5-8 minutes and you will see the dough starting to form again. Do not let it rest during the knead, as it will cause your dough to break apart. After kneading, your dough will have a smooth surface and will be less sticky than before.

6. Now, place your palms on the sides of your dough and rotate it with your fingers, forming a beautiful boule and tightening the dough's surface. Pick up the dough with the help of a lightly floured bench scraper, place it in a bowl, cover with a damp kitchen towel, and let it rise for an hour and a half or until it doubles in size at room temperature.

7. Now, with the back of your hand, lightly punch down the dough to let out some the gas that has developed. Then, flour your work surface again and dump the dough back on it. Now, with the help of your bench scraper, roughly divide the dough into eight different parts, weighing approximately 70-80 grams each.

8. Similar to the method used to shape the original dough into a boule, individually shape each of the eight pieces into small boules and set aside. Find a metal baking sheet that can accommodate all of your boules and lightly grease it by rubbing it with butter or by using a cooking spray.

9. Then, gently lift the boules into the pan, space them apart evenly, and cover with a damp towel to prove for a couple of hours at room temperature or until doubled in size. Beat your egg for the egg wash and add the milk, mixing thoroughly. Gently use a kitchen brush to coat the surface of your boules lightly, making sure to cover the entire surface.

10. Preheat your oven to 175°C (350°F) for an hour and then place the baking sheet with your boules inside for 25-30 minutes until the tops are a beautiful golden brown and the internal temperature of the bun registers at around 98°C (210°F). Bring the finished rolls out and let them rest for a while. You can tear into them right away, and they will still taste amazing. Make sure to serve them with a generous serving of butter on the top.

Rye Loaf Recipe

Ingredients:

Levain:

- **50 grams of Mature Sourdough Starter:** Make sure that you have fed the starter the day before.
- **250 grams of Dark Rye Flour:** Dark rye flour is the darker variant of the flour made from rye berries. The darker color is due to the higher amount of bran being present in the flour. Use organic unbleached flour.
- **250 grams of Water:** Make sure the water is unfiltered and at room temperature.

Dough:

- **550 grams of Levain**
- **175 grams of Whole Wheat Flour:** Whole wheat flour consists of the entire wheat kernel.
- **175 Grams of Dark Rye Flour**
- **275 grams of Water:** Make sure the water is unfiltered and at room temperature.
- **15 grams of Salt:** Use a non-iodized salt, like sea salt, and make sure it has fine grains.
- **2 Tablespoons of Caraway:** These will enhance the flavor of the bread, but they are optional.

Steps:

1. Start by taking a clean, dry glass jar and place it on the weighing scale, making sure to use the tare option. Make sure the mature starter has at least doubled in size and has a bubbly and convex surface. Add the mature starter, flour, and water in that order and combine them with a flexible spatula until no dry bits are present and it forms a uniform paste. Cover with a loose-fitting lid and place it in a warm environment for 5-7 hours or until its surface starts to fall.

2. An hour before the levain has matured, add the flours one by one to a clean mixing bowl. To make it easier, place it on the weighing scale and use the tare option to reset the scale. Mix the flours gently with your hand. Now, check the temperature of your water, making sure it lies between 27-29°C (80-85°F) and heat if necessary. Add it to the mixing bowl and form a cohesive dough mixture, making sure to leave no dry clumps. Cover with a dampened towel and leave it to rest for at least 45 minutes to autolyze.

3. Once the dough mixture has autolyzed, add the levain to the mix along with the caraway seeds and salt and mix it thoroughly until combined. You can also lift the dough from one side and slap it back down in the bowl repeatedly for better results. The dough will be more of a thick paste rather than the traditional consistency from other recipes because of the low gluten content of rye. Again, cover and let it sit for an hour.

4. Over two hours, perform a set of four very gentle stretch and folds. The dough will stretch only a little, so keep in mind not to break it. Read the previous section for an insight into the process, and you will notice the dough becomes slightly smoother during the process. Cover again, let the dough ferment for 2-2.5 hours, and rest the dough in the same warm environment as your starter and levain.

5. After the ferment, the surface of your dough should be bubbly and have developed some cracks. Lightly flour your work surface and dump the mixture gently onto it, taking care not to degas it. Press gently on the dough and shape it into the rough form that is the length and width of your loaf pan. You can do this by gently flattening the dough into a square the length of the loaf pan, and then rolling it upon itself until it manages to fit snugly into the loaf pan.

6. Coat the inside of your loaf pan with butter or a cooking spray and gently place the dough inside. You can do this with lightly floured hands, as the dough will not be that sticky. Cover the pan with a damp towel and let it rest again in the warm environment for two hours to proof.

7. After the proof, your dough should have risen considerably and developed a bubbly texture. Now, preheat the oven at 232°C (450°F) for at least an hour. If your loaf pan does not come with a lid, place an ovenproof bowl lined with foil inside the oven while preheating. Once preheated, bake with the lid on at the same temperature for 20 minutes. In the case of no lid, place 10-15 ice cubes into the ovenproof dish, and follow the same instructions. After that, remove the lid or the ice and bake for another 20 minutes until a deep golden-brown crust develops and a thermometer registers the internal temperature at 98°C (210°F). Remove and place your bread on a wire rack, letting it cool down to room temperature.

Bread-Making Process Non-Yeast Leavened

The steps below go over bread that does not utilize natural yeast but instead, uses a chemical leavening agent. Also, we have included flatbreads, most of which skip the leavening altogether. Go through the steps to get a general understanding of the process so you can be confident when you try out a recipe on your own.

Non-Yeast Bread Baking Process in 4 Steps

1. Mixing Ingredients
Like the previous method, you will need to weigh each ingredient individually, making sure the they are all at room temperature. Mixing the ingredients will vary across recipes, so read the instructions on which ingredients you need to add first. Mix with your hands and then proceed to the next step.

2. Kneading
Now, you will need to knead your dough to develop the gluten. You will have to either use your hands in the steps mentioned previously or use a stand mixer with the dough attachment. Keep in mind that some recipes will ask you to add additional ingredients during or after the kneading process. You will notice that the dough's surface will become smooth and less sticky.

3. Shaping/Rolling
Now, you will continue on to the process of giving the final shape to your bread. In the flatbread's case, you will need to roll out the dough into a thin sheet using a rolling pin. For non-yeast leavened bread, like soda bread, you would shape it according to the form you want. Also, score the surface of your dough if directed to do so in the recipe.

4. Cooking/Baking
Most flatbreads cook on a pan and do not require an oven. Follow the recipe instructions to learn about the proper method for each type. For the non-yeast leavened bread, follow the same baking process as the previous section states, in addition to setting the

temperature according to the recipe. Also, you might not need to steam the oven in some recipes, but be sure to cover your bread when baking it to prevent it from burning.

Yeast-Free Bread Recipes

Soda Bread Recipe

Ingredients:

- **400 ml of Buttermilk:** Buttermilk is a sour liquid that is typically fermented or cultured milk. You can get this from any nearby store. Do not substitute this with milk since the baking soda needs buttermilk to activate.
- **255 grams of All-Purpose Flour:** All-purpose flour is a type of wheat flour where the bran of the wheat grain is absent. For the best results, make sure the flour you use is unbleached.
- **255 grams of Whole Wheat Flour:** Whole wheat flour consists of the entire wheat kernel.
- **40 grams of Butter:** Make sure the butter is as cold as possible. You can use butter directly from the fridge or keep the butter in the freezer for 10 minutes before using it.
- **1 large Egg**
- **1 Teaspoon of Baking Soda:** Make sure that the baking soda is fresh and measured to the exact amount mentioned.
- **1 Teaspoon of Salt**
- **3 Tablespoons of Granulated Sugar:** You can determine if the sugar is granulated if it has a crystalline form.

Steps:

1. Take a clean, dry mixing bowl and add the flours, salt, baking soda, and sugar, then mix them with the help of a whisk or spoon until thoroughly combined. Now, add the cubes of butter into your flour and with the help of your fingertips, incorporate the butter until the mixture resembles breadcrumbs.

2. In a separate bowl, whisk the egg and buttermilk until the mixture has a uniform color. Now, gradually add the liquid mixture into the mixing bowl containing the dry ingredients and mix with your hands until a dough forms. Stop adding the liquid mixture if the dough becomes too watery or sticky and make sure that there are no dry bits of flour left in the bowl.

3. Now, flour a work surface like a kitchen counter, dump the dough onto it, and make sure not to leave any residue in the bowl. If the dough is sticky, add a little bit of flour. Now, use your hands to knead the dough gently for 30 seconds to help it form.

4. After forming, gently work the dough into an 8-inch circular loaf with the help of your fingers. Once the dough forms, transfer the dough onto a metal baking sheet lined with flour with the help of a floured metal bench scraper.

5. Preheat your oven to 200°C (400°F) for at least an hour. Before placing the loaf into the oven, take a sharp knife and make two cuts across the dough's surface perpendicular to one another so that they resemble a cross shape. Lightly beat an egg and brush the surface of your dough, making sure to leave no area exposed.

6. Place the dough in the oven and bake it at 200°C (400°F) for 30-45 minutes until there is a beautiful golden-brown surface and the center of your loaf registers at a temperature of 98°C (210°F). Let the bread cool for an hour or until it reaches room temperature and then cut it into slices and enjoy.

Cornbread Recipe – Gluten Free

Ingredients:

- **280 grams of Finely Ground Cornmeal:** Cornmeal is a flour made from dried corn. Make sure to use the finest variety possible. You can also use 140 grams of all-purpose flour and cornmeal each if you do not desire a gluten-free bread.
- **85 grams of Unsalted Butter**
- **300 ml of Buttermilk:** Buttermilk is a sour liquid that is typically fermented or cultured milk. You can get this from any nearby store. Do not substitute this with milk since the baking soda needs buttermilk to activate.
- **15 grams of Sugar**
- **1 Teaspoon of Salt**
- **1 Teaspoon Baking Powder**
- **1 Large Egg**

Steps:

1. Place a 9 to 10-inch cast iron pan or ovenproof dish in an oven and preheat at 200°C (392°F). Now, take a medium saucepan and add your butter. Place it over medium heat and let it melt completely. After the butter melts, continue heating until it starts to brown, making sure to swirl the saucepan consistently. Once you notice some brown bits settling to the bottom, remove the pan from the heat. Pour the butter into a heatproof container and let it cool down completely.

2. Now, add your dry ingredients, which are the cornmeal, sugar, salt, and baking powder. Whisk and combine until the mixture is homogeneous. In a different bowl, whisk up the egg and gradually add in your buttermilk while continuously whisking. Then, add the brown butter slowly while continuing to whisk the mixture.

3. Now, add the liquid mixture to the dry ingredients and mix with a whisk until a thick and homogenous mixture forms. Take out your pan from the oven and coat the surface lightly with butter or cooking oil. Add your cornbread mixture directly to the hot pan and even the surface to make it smooth with the help of a spatula.

4. Place the pan back into the oven and cook at 200°C (392°F) for 20 minutes. Check for doneness by inserting a toothpick at the center and seeing if it comes out clean. Let the bread rest in the pan for 15-20 minutes or until it reaches room temperature. Cut into even wedges and serve.

Tortilla Recipe

Ingredients:

- **245 grams of All-Purpose Flour:** All-purpose flour is a type of wheat flour where the bran of the wheat grain is absent. For the best results, make sure the flour you use is unbleached.
- **177 grams of Water:** Make sure the water is warm, at about 43°C (110°F).
- **1 Teaspoon of Baking Powder:** Make sure that the baking soda is fresh and measured to the exact amount mentioned.
- **3 Tablespoons of Oil:** Tortillas traditionally use lard, but you can substitute it with any neutral-tasting oil.
- **1/2 Teaspoon of Salt**

Steps:

1. Take a mixing bowl and make sure it is clean and dry. Add the flour, salt, and baking soda, then mix by hand or with the help of a whisk until a consistent mixture forms. Now, if you are using lard, add it to the mixture and use your fingers to gently rub it in until the mixture resembles cornmeal.

2. Now, add the water to the flour. If using cooking oil, add it into the mixture along with the water. Mix thoroughly with your hands until a shaggy dough forms.

3. Gently dust a work surface, like your kitchen countertop, and dump the dough onto it. Knead lightly for a few minutes, making sure to frequently change the direction you knead until the surface of the dough becomes smooth and elastic.

4. Now, lightly flour the surface of the dough and cover with a dampened kitchen towel or inverted bowl for 10-15 minutes.

After resting, divide the dough into 10-15 pieces, which weigh approximately 30-40 grams each.

5. Now, roll each piece into a nice even ball with the help of your fingers and lay them on your work surface. Preheat a cast-iron skillet over medium-high heat for at least 10 minutes until the surface is ripping hot.

6. Again, flour your work surface and work each dough ball into an even circle with a rolling pin. Make sure to use a floured rolling pin to prevent the dough from sticking. To get an even roundness, you can turn the dough by about a quarter every time you roll it out. Roll it to 1/8th of an inch thick.

7. You can also use a tortilla press to get the desired shape. Just place the ball in the center, close the lid tightly, and then open the press to get a perfectly formed dough.

8. Gently place the rolled-out dough onto the surface of your skillet and leave it on the heat until it becomes bubbly and the surface touching the heat develops some charred brown spots. This should take approximately 25-30 seconds. Once done, flip the tortilla with a flat-headed spatula and let the other side also develop a proper char.

9. Remove the tortilla from the pan, place it on a plate, and cover with aluminum foil to retain the heat. Repeat the same steps for the remaining tortillas.

Troubleshooting Tips

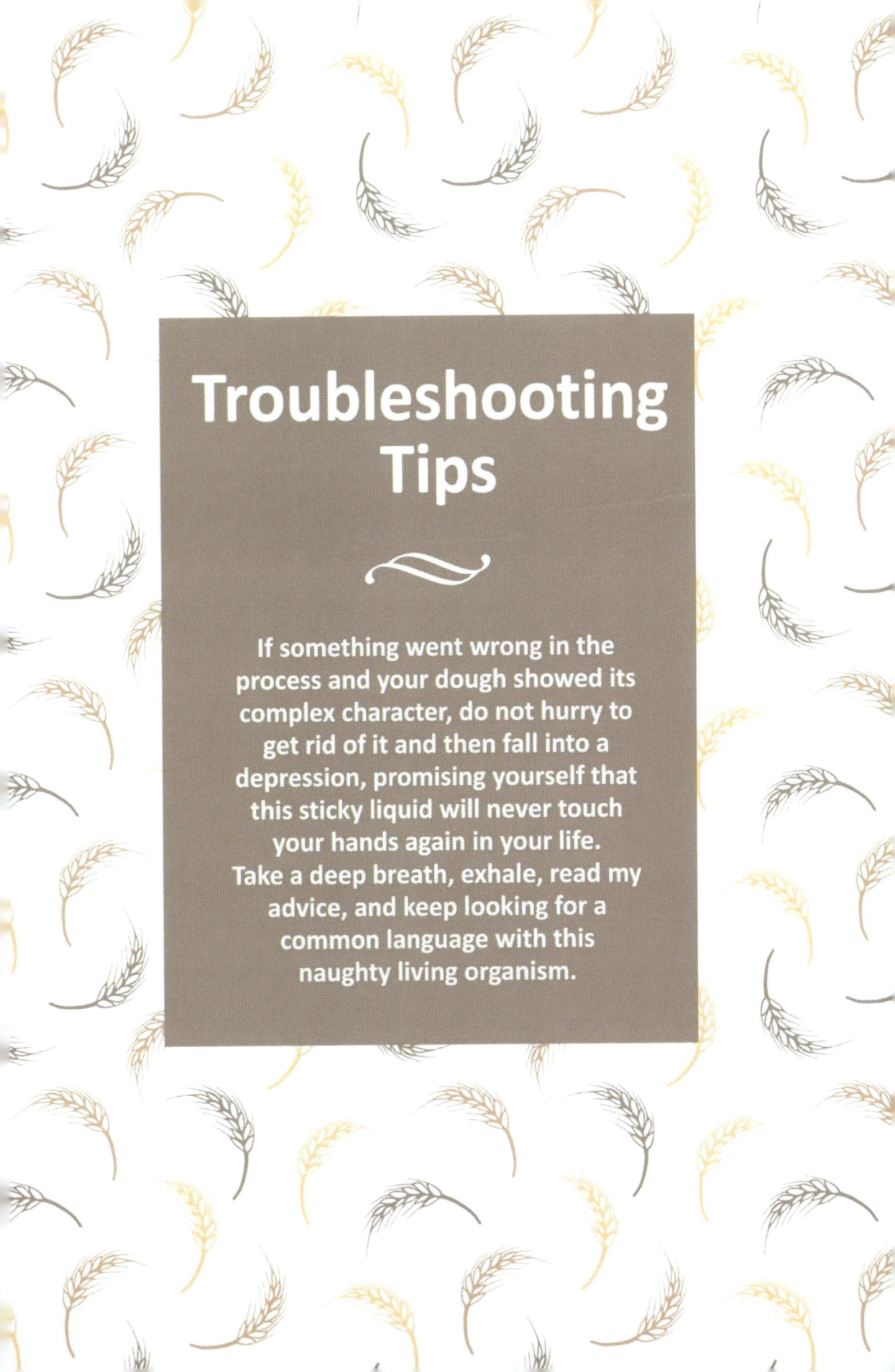

~

If something went wrong in the process and your dough showed its complex character, do not hurry to get rid of it and then fall into a depression, promising yourself that this sticky liquid will never touch your hands again in your life. Take a deep breath, exhale, read my advice, and keep looking for a common language with this naughty living organism.

Milk Rolls

The yeast milk mixture shows no sign of activity: This can mean that your yeast has expired or that the milk's temperature is too low. Try again until you get a bubbly mixture.

The dough starts breaking while kneading: While kneading in the butter, the dough can break up. If you experience this, continue kneading for an additional 5-6 minutes until the dough combines and becomes smooth.

The baking dish is not large enough: In this case, roll out all your boules, fit what you can on the baking dish, and place the remaining dough in plastic wrap in the fridge. After baking the first batch, remove, let it warm to room temperature, and repeat the process until you finish your dough.

Rye Bread

The dough is not forming together: Rye flour has a low gluten content, which means that it will not hold itself together like regular wheat flour. Try increasing the wheat flour percentage slightly the next time you make the recipe for an easier knead.

The dough is too sour: If the dough is too sour for your taste, you can reduce the amount of time your starter rests after feeding it. Rye flour will generally have a more sour taste due to yeast's better growth when fed with it.

Soda Bread

Buttermilk is unavailable: If you do not have buttermilk on hand, a good alternative is to replace it by mixing 400 ml of skimmed milk with a teaspoon of vinegar or lemon juice. Whisk together in a measuring cup and leave it for five minutes.

The dough is sticky: The main reason could be that the butter used is not cold enough. The next time you make the bread, ensure that your butter is as cold as possible. Also, confirm that your buttermilk mixture is cool.

Tortillas

The tortillas are brittle: For the best results, use cold hardened lard and knead the dough thoroughly for at least five minutes to get soft tortillas. You can also add a little bit of oil to coat the surface of your pan while cooking the tortillas.

The tortillas burn up: Your pan may have become too hot. Make sure to keep your skillet at medium-high heat. If it still burns, consider reducing the heat for the next batch.

Cornbread

The cornbread is crumbly: The main reason for this is the lack of gluten due to the absence of gluten in cornbread. You can reduce the amount of corn flour by half and substitute it with all-purpose flour. Keep in mind that this will remove the bread's gluten-free status.

The butter bursts out of the pan while boiling: The main reason for this could be that you are not swirling the saucepan sufficiently. Make sure to consistently swirl to prevent the butter from bursting out.

The Bread Didn't Work: 17 Reasons Why

1. The dough is too sticky/watery
Before the stretch and fold, if you notice the mixture is fluid or not workable, you can add a bit of flour to make the dough more comfortable to handle.

2. The dough does not increase during bulk ferment
The primary reason for a lack of a sufficient rise during the bulk ferment has to do with your sourdough starter. The next time you bake bread, ensure that you have fed your starter the day before using it and that its surface is convex and bubbly. If your starter does not rise, continue feeding it every twelve hours for a couple of days and place it in a warm environment until it shows activity.

3. The bread's bottom has browned considerably
You can place the Dutch oven or bowl, wherever your dough rests, over an aluminum foil-lined baking sheet to prevent the bottom from burning.

4. The crumb is too dense
The secret to an airy loaf lies in rising your dough when fermenting and proofing. For the best results, use an active sourdough starter and be careful while shaping to prevent the formed bubbles in the dough from degassing. You can also ferment your dough and starter in a warmer area. Another possible reason could be that you have under-proofed your dough. Let the dough prove for an extra hour the next time before you bake your bread.

5. The starter or dough is covered with a dense crust

First of all, you should carefully cover it with a thick towel. You can even moisten it and if it is near the battery, move it aside and find a less dry but warm place if possible.

6. The dough becomes covered with a network of cracks during proofing

The problem is also insufficient moisture. It is necessary to ensure good moistening of the upper crust; wet it before proofing, cover with a damp towel during the proofing period, and wet the towel again as it dries.

7. The top crust turns out to be thick and tough during baking

The problem, of course, may be in violation of the baking mode; the initial heat or baking temperature were too high or the time spent baking was too long. Or perhaps, the problem lies in the drying of the crust during proofing once again. In this case, proceed as described in the previous paragraph.

8. The bread is not understood and has a loose crumb

Let's describe this disgrace: the crumb is dense, and in places that it is moist and very dense, almost stuck, it also has large, rough pores. In the case of rye dough, these will not be oversized pores, but instead, it will have a heavily exfoliated upper or lower crust, in addition to large rough cracks on the outside and sometimes on the inside of the bread. Wheat bread usually has a bland, unexpressed taste or an acidic and sour taste with bitterness. Also, the crumb is coarse and rubbery, and the crust is ugly.

Reasons: The starter may be to blame; it neither loosened the dough nor saturated it with gas. Perhaps it got weaker every day (for example, in the refrigerator), or raw materials (for example, poor quality flour) are to blame.

Perhaps you did not let the sourdough or dough ripen and you used it before it became fluffy. The activity of the dough directly depends on how the starter has matured. The word "ripened" means how much accumulation has occurred in the culture; such as yeast and lactic acid bacteria for fermentation and the loosening of the dough. If the dough didn't become lush and didn't sag in the middle, it's not enough. If it's lush and slightly sagged, it's ready! Moreover, if there are no splendor and bubbles, then it is too early. And lastly, too late means it was allowed to ferment too long before the accumulation of a lot of acids and the destruction of gluten.

Another reason for a loose crumb is coldness! It's cool in the kitchen, so the fermentation temperature has dropped, which makes the dough ferment slower. If you do not pay attention to this and to the state of the dough, you may not notice that the dough has not yet come up, that it needs a little more time, and that you need to shape it earlier than necessary or bake it before the dough becomes loosened and fluffy.

9. Sour bread

The reason for the excess acidity in the taste is a weak starter. For some reason, the yeast in your starter is weak and slow, and lactic acid bacteria are faster and accumulate a lot of acids. If your starter is healthy and active, but you overexposed it, then the dough becomes overripe and when it ferments, there will be sourness but it will still be healthy and tasty. Unhealthy sourness is immediately detectable: it is pungent with a bitter aftertaste, and, if such is observed, the reason is in the weak starter.

10. The top of the bread has settled

You take the bread out of the oven and it has a sagging top, or you put it in the oven and saw how it fell off during the baking process. There are several scenarios for the development of these events, and the reasons are basically the same: the bread is fermented. This means that at the stage of the final proofing, just before baking, the dough fermented for too long. As a result of which, a lot of gas accumulated in the dough and the gluten was too weak, for it became flabby and lost the ability to maintain its elastic shape. In simple words: it fermented and stopped. If this happens, reduce the proofing of the dough by 20 minutes, or lower the fermentation temperature by 2-3 degrees.

11. The surface of the bread is severely torn

You baked bread but it was torn very badly. Usually, a little more rubber crumb is attached to such a crust, seemingly loosened, but in this situation, it seems that something is missing. Also, there can be many pores inside the bread, but oddly enough, they are all narrow and vertical. The reason for this defect is the opposite of the previous one: insufficient proofing.

If you can easily cope with the past problem (the dough has fermented) by reducing the proving time, then this will prove to be a more difficult challenge, as there may be several reasons. The dough might not have had enough time to prove simply because the room was cool or your starter culture was running slower. Or, it may be that you did not let the dough come up during fermentation (that is, during the fermentation that follows immediately after kneading) before molding and waiting for proofing.

So, the better the dough is at the fermentation stage, the faster the proofing will be. If you begin to divide and mold before the dough is fluffy, the dough will take longer to come up. In such cases, focus on the dough through feel, taste, and listen. This is the only truly effective way to understand the dough: to listen to what it tells and shows you, which we talked about in more detail above.

12. The crumb turns out to be denser than you want, the middle is dense too

A few reasons:
- ✓ Rough molding with pressure in the center results in a denser crumb in the middle, which needs more time to prove than the outer layers that do not have as much, so they do not have time to open and turn out denser. To solve this, exit, learn to shape, exercise, and do not press the middle of the dough! If the dough diverges during molding, moisten it so that it sticks to itself better and make sure that there is not an excessive amount of flour on the dough during molding.
- ✓ There was not enough oven heat for the existing workpiece so the edges opened up and the middle remained rather dense. The workpiece, getting into the oven, immediately begins to warm up, but it happens unevenly: first, the outer layers, next, the thin edges, and lastly, the dense middle is warmed up.
- ✓ You did not let the bread ferment well enough after kneading at the fermentation stage, so therefore, you began to mold too early.

13. Bread spreads in the oven

✓ If it just spreads and does not deflate, then, most likely, the reason is weak mixing and weak molding. You need to understand that gluten can keep the shape of the bread and prevent the dough from spreading, but we first develop gluten in a batch. The dough, which is poorly kneaded and not elastic tears when stretched, sticks, and is impossible to form a good workpiece from. With such a dough, the cuts will not open the cuts and instead, will simply give away. A good workpiece is when the surface of the dough is well stretched and feels elastic to the touch but is also soft inside, retaining its splendor. In many ways, it is the stretched surface of the workpiece that makes it so that it does not blur immediately after it is taken out of the basket.

✓ Another reason the bread spreads is the low baking temperature. The temperature in the oven may not be enough to grab the crust. Therefore, the bread is baked with smaller pores and less volume.

14. Bread crumbles

If your bread crumbles when slicing, the main reasons are either a too weak or too intense mix, but the bottom line is the lack of gluten, bread's weakness. And, this weakness can be caused by either excessive kneading and the destruction of gluten or by under-mixing and the underdevelopment of gluten. The elasticity of the dough (the ability to stretch and regain its previous shape, to hold a large amount of gas inside, and to form the dough frame) is largely the merit of gluten. If this suffers, then you will get a sticky and too extensible dough, a low volume of bread, and, as a result, a fragile dough frame that collapses during the baking process. This means that the gluten threads and films that hold the gas are destroyed, the pores break, and the bread crumbles when cutting. If you have not kneaded the dough, then roughly the same thing happens with the same crumbliness. However, the destruction of gluten bonds does not occur due to mixing or overheating, but instead because they did not develop in the batch and could not properly stretch in the period of bread growth in the oven and therefore broke.

15. The crust of the bread cracks has many small cracks

If your bread comes out with a lot of small cracks, then you are most likely dealing with a sticky, weak dough or a dough with a lot of rye or gluten-free flour. As with a fragile crumb, multiple crust cracks are the result of poor gluten.

16. The bread comes out with a coarse thick crust without beautiful cuts, or with torn cuts, or does not open in the cuts

I must say that such a crust does not smell very tasty, at least, not at all like a golden thin crust smells. So, the crust does not smell because it did not have enough moisture in the first 15 minutes of baking. In general, a lack of steam in a bread oven has a whole spectrum of manifestations: the cuts do not open, but instead freeze, and the bread breaks from the side or in any unexpected place, but not where you slashed it with a blade. Also, the crust is not gilded, does not have a saturated color, but as it turns out, is gray, whitish, or matte. All this is from a lack of steam, and if you thought you had already created it in your oven, put bowls of water on the bottom of the oven, as you are mistaken since the crust says otherwise.

The oven should have a powerful steam boost, which can be created either by the bread itself under a hot bell, by boiling water that you splash on a hot pan, or by something else that must lead to an active powerful evaporation of moisture in the oven, such as ice.

17. The incisions float and the crust glistens

You need lots of steam! You can also shorten the hydration time or the amount of hydration water!

As a result, I want to say that we have now considered all these defects and causes separately from each other. However, each problem relates and affects one another, so try to consider any defect not in itself, but in context. This means that apart from some major defects, pay attention to all aspects: crust, crumb, taste, crust breaks, color, crumb structure, fermentation time, temperature, dough behavior, etc. Analyze the whole picture!

Conclusion

So, my friend, now you know where to start, what will be useful for you, how to choose flour, how to grow a starter, how to knead, and how to bake bread. I hope that now you are not afraid of words like "proofing" or "autolysis." I think I saved you a lot of time and effort, and now you can bake bread with ease. The main thing is to be patient, follow all the steps, and do not panic if something goes wrong. Instead, just read my advice and try again. Let this book be the beginning of your great passion for baking!

Bonus pages

Type of flour (100 g)	Benefits	Contraindications	Gluten	Cal	Prot., Fats, Carbs.	Glycemic index
Wheat flour	Positive impact on the functioning of the nervous system, activation of mental functions, and replenishment of energy and strength. The condition of hair, skin, nails and blood improve. General well-being is stabilized.	Increase in body weight. It is forbidden to include in diets with gluten intolerance, diabetes, obesity, allergies, or high blood pressure.	Yes	364	10.0 1.0 76.0	85
Whole wheat flour	Improves digestive processes, prevents obesity and atherosclerosis, and removes toxins and heavy metals from the body. This flour, with proper nutrition, does not allow weight to increase, but, actually helps reduce it. The levels of bad cholesterol and sugar do not rise.	Exacerbation of chronic gastrointestinal diseases. Therefore, it is not recommended to use it for diseases of the stomach, intestines, liver, and pancreas. Prohibition for dysbiosis.	Yes	331	11.3 2.2 60.2	65
Rye flour	Supports well-being during intense sports training, increases energy expenditure, and decreases body fat. Maintains normal blood cholesterol levels. Development of resistance to stress.	Flatulence, digestive disorders. In case of gluten intolerance or exacerbation of gastrointestinal tract disease, do not use.	Yes	297	8.7 1.7 62.0	40
Rye bran	Strengthens immunity and increases the body's resistance to various colds and infectious diseases. Cleanses the body of toxins, normalizes blood sugar levels, and removes salts of heavy metals, radionuclides, and carcinogens from the body.	Not recommended for use by people suffering from diarrhea, gastritis, stomach ulcers, and gastrointestinal erosion.	Yes	114	12.2 3.4 8.7	25
Buckwheat flour	Replenishes energy reserves, strengthens immunity, and normalizes	Allergy or individual intolerance to vegetable protein.	No	344	13.7 1.5 70.8	50

	the course of nervous processes and blood circulation. The skin, hair, and nails are improved, excess cholesterol is removed, and thyroid function is supported.	Forbidden for Crohn's disease and irritable bowel syndrome.				
Flaxseed flour	Strengthens the immune defense, improves well-being, activates metabolic processes, and normalizes the digestive tract. There is a positive effect on the heart, blood vessels, hormones, and nervous system. Cholesterol and blood sugar are stabilized, and toxic substances are eliminated.	Bloating, flatulence, indigestion. It is forbidden for kidney stones, gall bladder, and thyroid problems. Use with diabetes is limited.	No	288	34.7 12.6 10.1	35
Oatmeal flour	Increased production of serotonin, the hormone of joy. This will give the desired mood to maintain diets and reduce the severity of hunger attacks. In addition, stress levels decrease, the functions of the gastrointestinal tract and liver are normalized, and the body is cleansed of "bad" cholesterol.	Eating too much oatmeal that is undercooked or raw can cause intestinal blockages and severe constipation. Oatmeal contains phytic acid. Phytates are chelated and render important nutrients unsuitable for the intestines. This mainly concerns calcium, magnesium, zinc, and iron. You need to use it in moderation.	No	357	12.2 6.5 64.2	45
Oat bran flour	Regulates the functioning of the intestines, improves the microflora of the colon, promotes the elimination of cholesterol, helps with weight loss, normalizes blood sugar, and detoxifies the body as a whole.	Bran can interfere with the absorption of certain drugs. Excessive consumption of bran can cause bloating. People suffering from ulcers and gastritis are not allowed to consume bran at all as fiber can aggravate their situation.	No	320	18.0 7.1 45.3	15

Almond flour	An antioxidant that cleanses the body of toxic substances, prolongs the life of cells and the body, and reduces the risk of developing various diseases. Useful for stabilizing the nervous system and relieving stress. Normalizes the work of the heart, kidneys, and liver. Improves human immunity by protecting the immune system from viruses and bacteria.	In case of excessive consumption, it can cause stagnation in the gastrointestinal tract. Almond flour may be contraindicated in people with heart disease due to its high content of essential oils. Almond powder is very high in calories and can lead to obesity when consumed in large quantities.	No	539	18.3 41.2 14.4	25
Barley flour	Normalizes metabolism, improves food processing, and assimilates useful components. Slow carbohydrates keep you energized for a long time and prevents blood sugar spikes. Muscles are toned, bones and teeth are strengthened, and immunity and brain activity are improved.	It is forbidden for these diseases of the gastrointestinal tract: ulcers, gastritis with high acidity, and cholecystitis. Threatens those with exacerbation.	No	290	10.3 1.1 59.2	60
Corn flour	Normalizes the functions of the nervous system, increases blood flow to the brain, stabilizes the heart and blood vessels, and improves digestion. Regeneration in tissues is accelerated and muscle growth is stimulated during intensive training. At the same time, fat cells break down and metabolism is activated.	This is forbidden for people with diseases of the gastrointestinal tract in an acute form and for those with problems with blood clotting. It is required to exclude from diets for diseases of the pancreas in order to reduce the load.	No	332	8.2 1.4 71.0	70
Rice flour	Cleanses the body of harmful substances, removes excess fluid, and replenishes energy reserves. Rice flour is gluten-free and is considered to be hypoallergenic. Suitable for	Increase in body weight in the absence of control over the volume of portions. It is prohibited in case of diabetes mellitus,	No	341	6.4 1.0 78.7	95

	those who find it difficult to eliminate sugar from the diet as rice flour reduces the need for sugary foods.	obesity, and tendency for hemorrhoids or constipation. In the presence of diseases of the gastrointestinal tract, liver, and kidneys, it is required to limit use.			
Banana flour	Improves intestinal processes, has a positive effect on digestive and immune problems, lowers blood cholesterol levels, reduces excess weight and associated risks to the heart, prevents insulin resistance as well as indirectly type 2 diabetes, improves mental well-being due to the presence of 5-hydroxytryptophan with an antidepressant effect, and assists the nervous and muscular systems.	Banana flour should be used with caution for those with a high level of potassium in the blood since there is also a lot of it in the product. Also not recommended for those with kidney disease.	No	350	2.4 0.0 82.7	30
Chickpea flour	Helps with recovery, accelerates metabolism, and helps in shedding extra pounds. The amino acid methionine improves the functioning of the central nervous system. Chickpea flour does not provoke surges in sugar and insulin.	Limit if you are prone to digestive disorders. Completely exclude in case of allergies, gout, ulcers, and diseases of the gastrointestinal tract and kidneys in an aggravated form.	No	389	21.0 6.4 49.1	35
Chestnut flour	Helps with mastitis and mastopathy. Increases vascular tone, stimulates the production of adrenal hormones, strengthens capillaries and vascular walls, relieves edema, and reduces lymph flow. Helps with the stagnation of the venous system, diarrhea, malaria, increased acidity of gastric juice, uterine bleeding, vasospasm,	It should be used with caution during pregnancy, breastfeeding, with hypotension, liver and kidney disease, constipation, menstrual irregularities, and in childhood. In some cases, chestnut preparations can cause nausea and	No	360	6.65 3.0 78.00	65

	neuralgia, tuberculosis, and other diseases.	heartburn. If side effects occur, the drug should be discontinued.				
Bird cherry flour	Has a positive effect on the work of the heart. The content of iron and magnesium is essential for blood formation. It is useful in diabetes mellitus, and it also improves immunity and metabolism. For men, this is the best way to get rid of diseases of the genitourinary system. For women, lentils help reduce the severity of premenstrual syndrome and eases the course of menopause. For a child's body, beans are of particular value, for they affect growth and brain activity.	Diseases of the digestive tract and organs. Not for children under 3-5 years old due to the instability of the intestinal flora. Exacerbation of arthrosis, gout, osteochondrosis, and urolithiasis. Purines in the composition stimulate the accumulation of uric acid in the joints and the deposition of calculi in the kidneys.	No	118	7.6 0.0 21.8	Low

FAHRENHEIT to CELCIUS (F to C)
500 F = 260 C
475 F = 245 C
450 F = 235 C
425 F = 220 C
400 F = 205 C
375 F = 190 C
350 F = 180 C
325 F = 160 C
300 F = 150 C
275 F = 135 C
250 F = 120 C
225 F = 107 C

CUPS to MILILITERS (cup to ml)
1 cup = 16 tablespoons = 48 teaspoons = 240 ml
3/4 cup = 12 tablespoons = 36 teaspoons = 180 ml
2/3 cup = 11 tablespoons = 32 teaspoons = 160 ml
1/2 cup = 8 tablespoons = 24 teaspoons = 120 ml
1/3 cup = 5 tablespoons = 16 teaspoons = 80 ml
1/4 cup = 4 tablespoons = 12 teaspoons = 60 ml
1 tablespoon = 15 ml
1 teaspoon = 5 ml

CUPS to FLUID OUNCES (cup to fl. oz)
1 cup = 8 fl oz
3/4 cup = 6 fl oz
2/3 cup = 5 fl oz
1/2 cup = 4 fl oz
1/3 cup = 3 fl oz
1/4 cup = 2 fl oz
1 tablespoon = 0.5 fl oz
1 fl oz = 2 tablespoons = 6 teaspoons

FLOUR (CUP to GRAMS)
1 cup flour = 140 grams
3/4 cup flour = 105 grams
2/3 cup flour = 95 grams
1/2 cup flour = 70 grams
1/3 cup flour = 50 grams
1/4 cup flour = 35 grams
1 tablespoon flour = grams

GRANULATED SUGAR (CUP to GRAMS)
1 cup sugar = 200 grams
3/4 cup sugar = 150 grams
2/3 cup sugar = 135 grams
1/2 cup sugar = 100 grams
1/3 cup sugar = 70 grams
1/4 cup sugar = 50 grams
1 tablespoon sugar = 15 grams

POWDERED SUGAR (CUP to GRAMS)
1 cup powdered sugar = 160 grams
3/4 cup powdered sugar = 120 grams
2/3 cup powdered sugar = 105 grams
1/2 cup powdered sugar = 80 grams
1/3 cup powdered sugar = 55 grams
1/4 cup powdered sugar = 40 grams
1 tablespoon powdered sugar = 10 grams
1 egg (without shell) = 50 grams

Relax pages

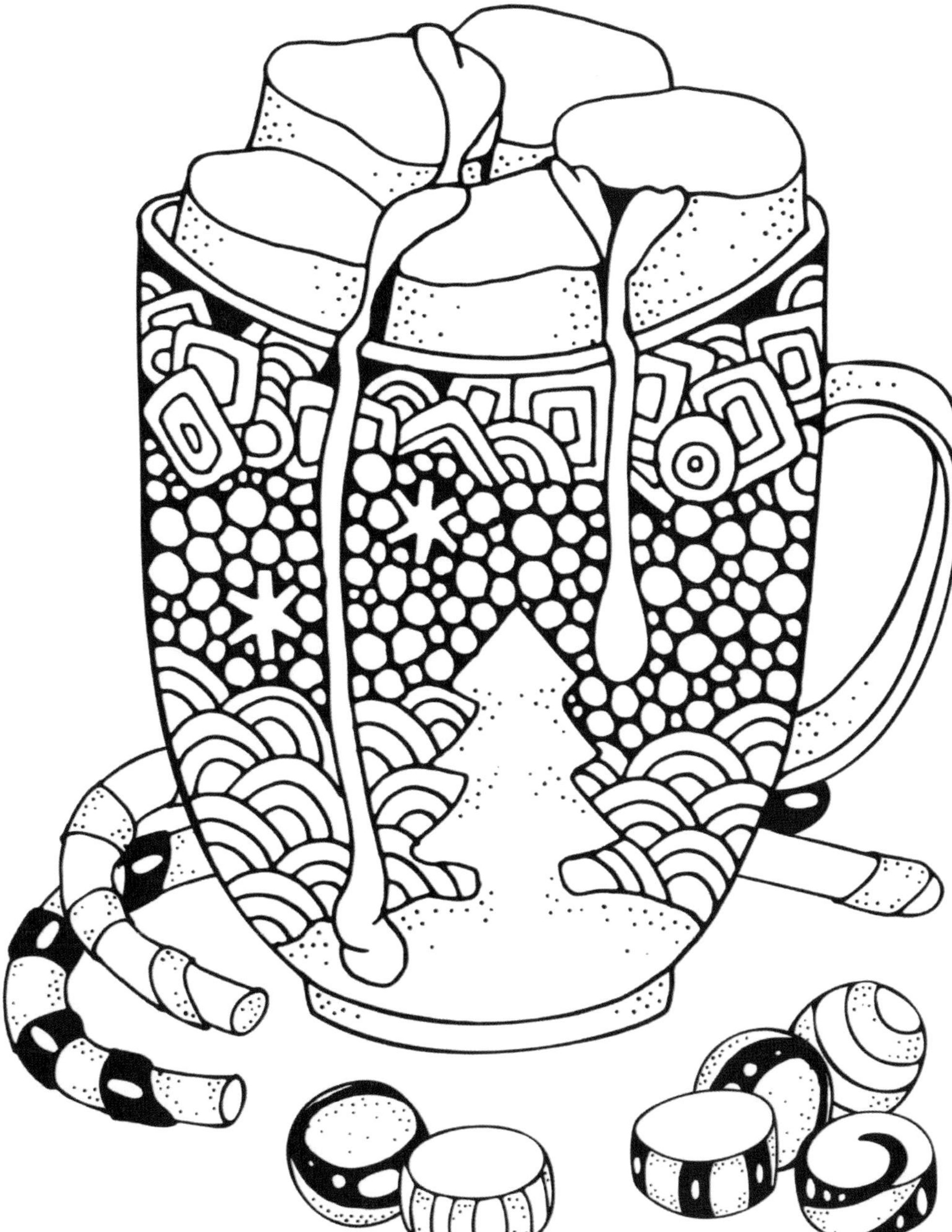

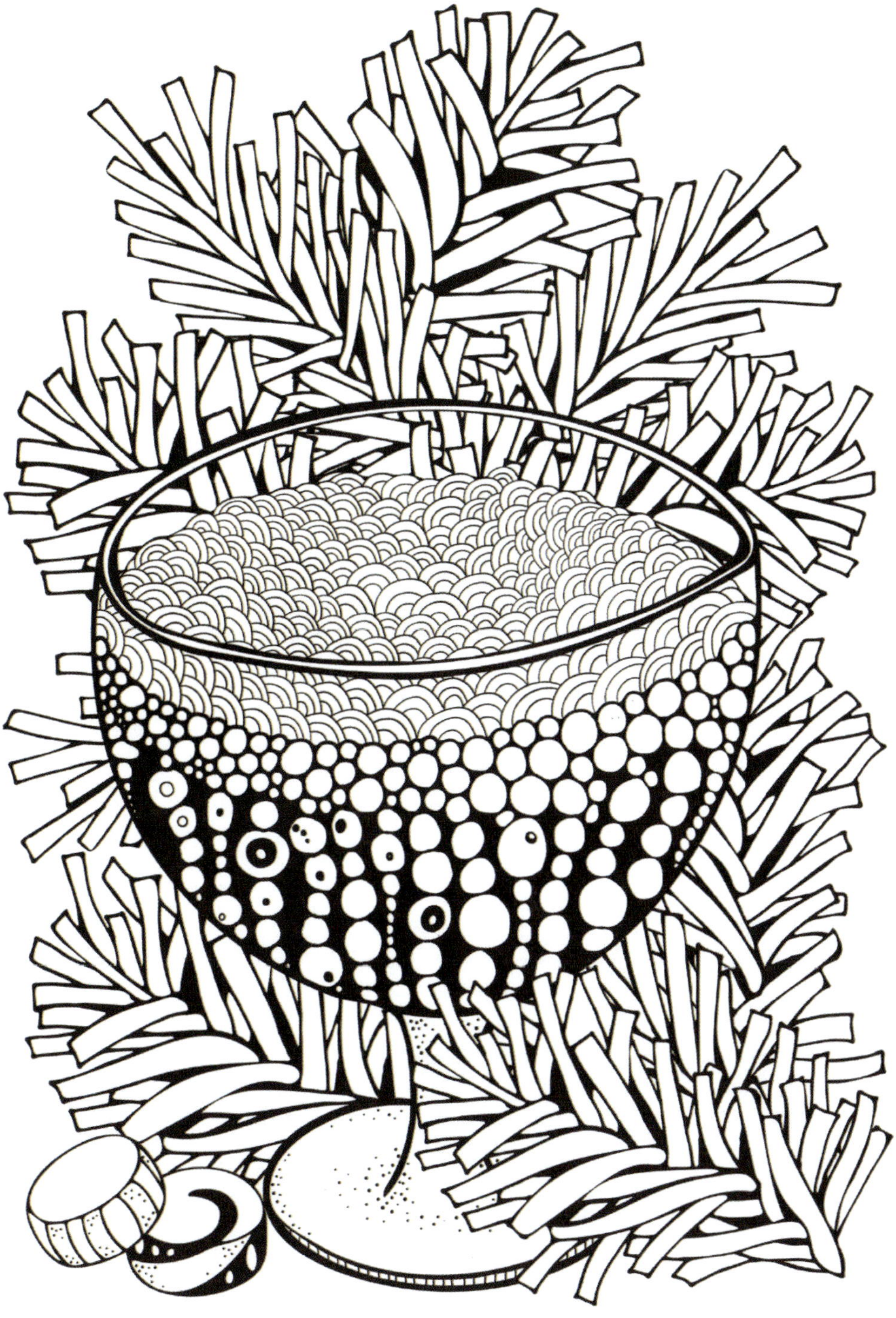

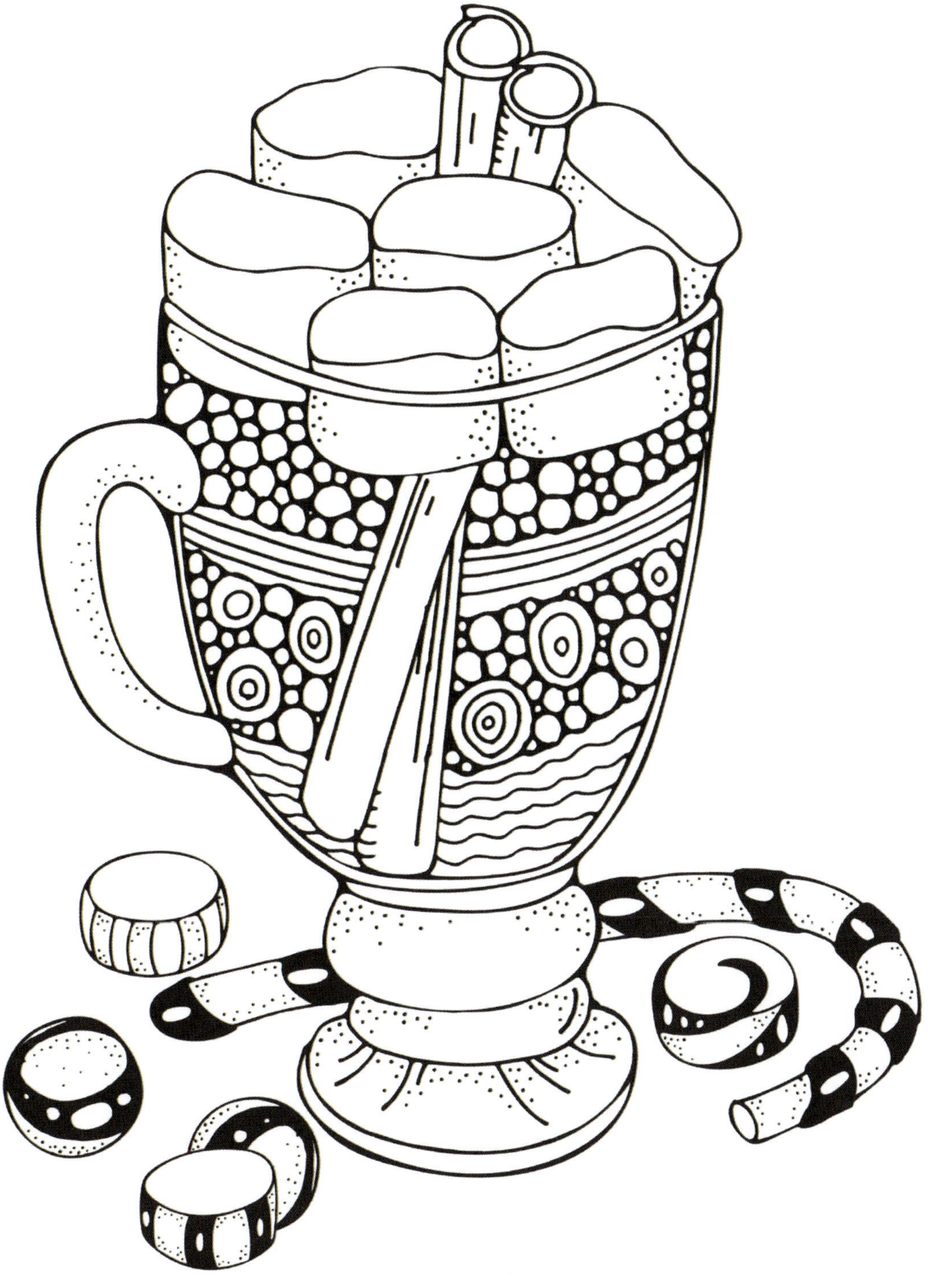

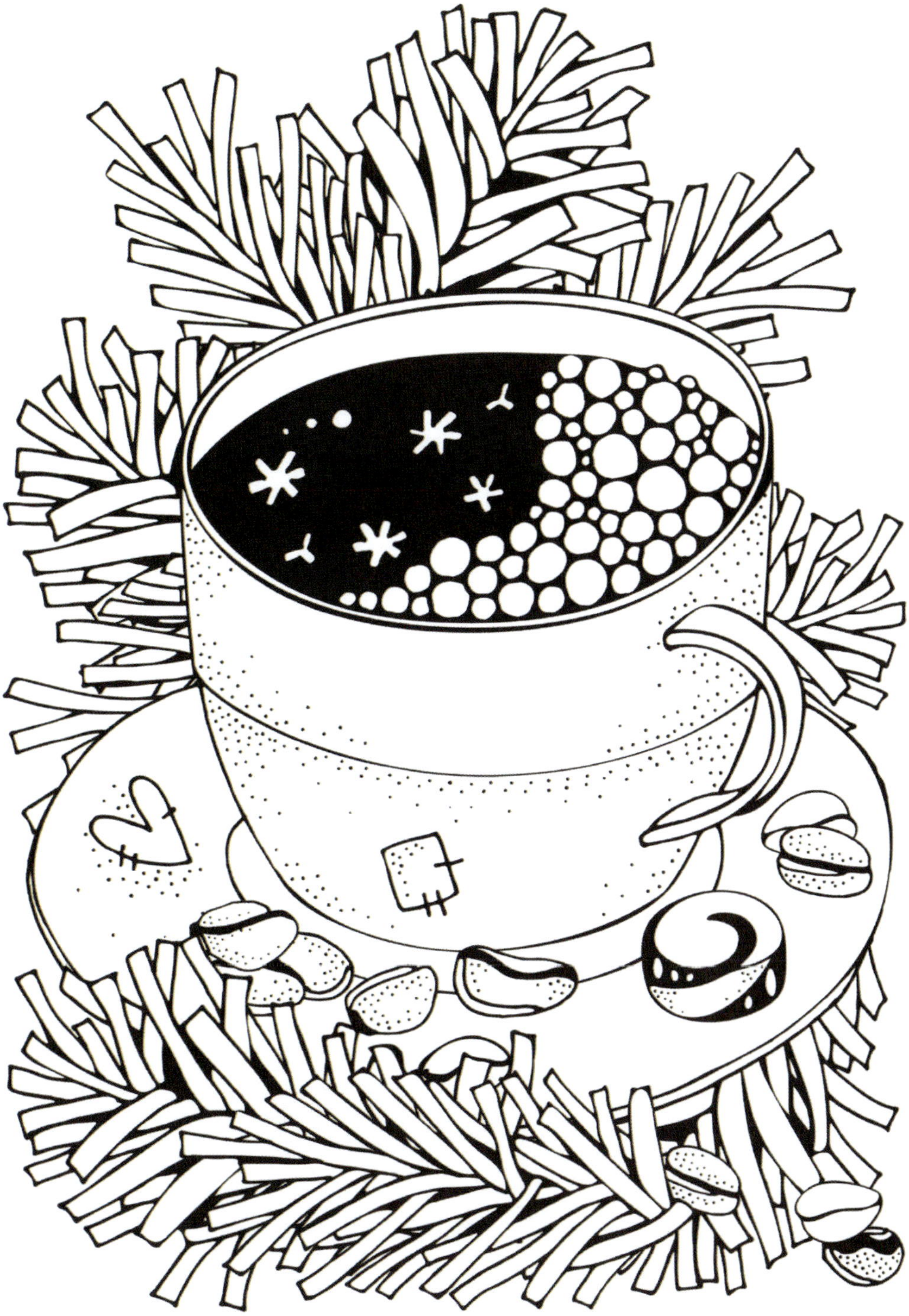

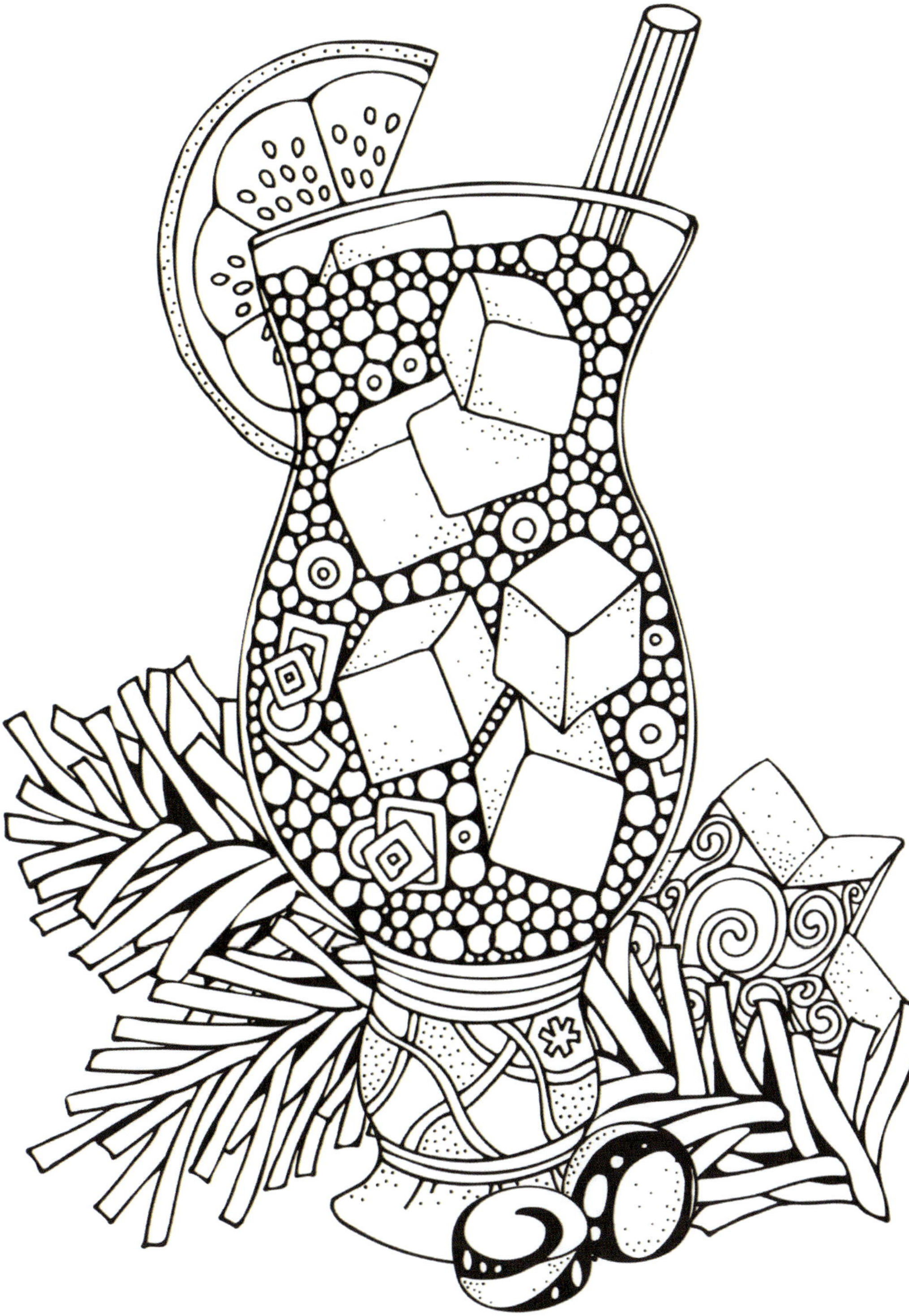

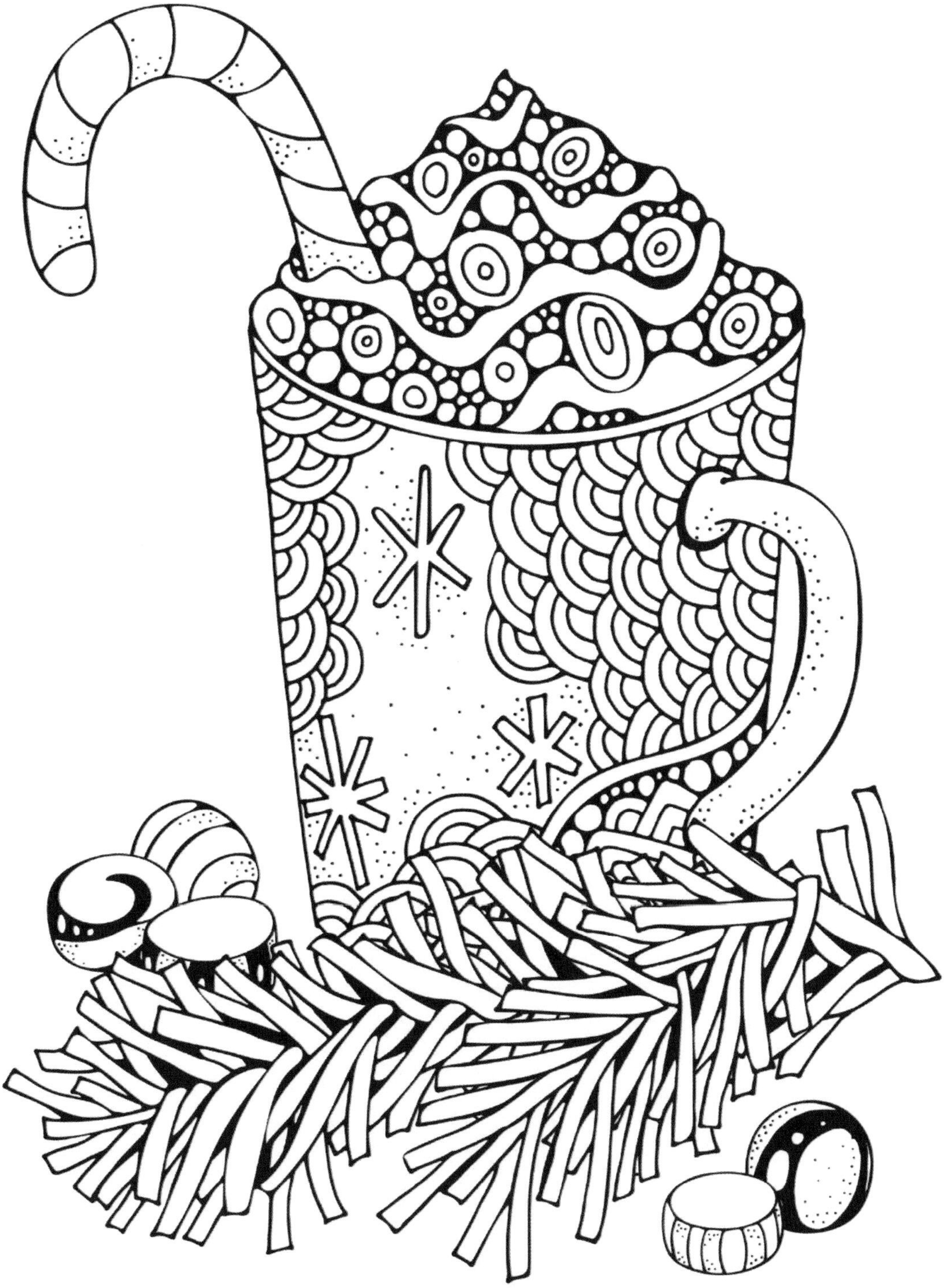

Printed in Great Britain
by Amazon